MEMORY AND HISTORY

Recollections of a Historian of Nazism, 1967-1982

Roderick Stackelberg

iUniverse, Inc.
Bloomington

Memory and History
Recollections of a Historian of Nazism, 1967-1982

iUniverse books may be ordered through booksellers or by contacting:

iUniverse
1663 Liberty Drive
Bloomington, IN 47403
www.iuniverse.com
1-800-Authors (1-800-288-4677)

ISBN: 978-1-4620-6442-7 (sc)
ISBN: 978-1-4620-6441-0 (hc)
ISBN: 978-1-4620-6440-3 (e)

Library of Congress Control Number: 2011960053

Printed in the United States of America

iUniverse rev. date: 11/10/2011

Contents

PREFACE

"Life is lived twice, once in the moment and again in retrospection." Anais Nin

"If you can't annoy somebody, there's little point in writing." Kingsley Amis

"We suppress an unpopular opinion, because we cannot afford the bitter cost of putting it forth. None of us likes to be hated, and none of us likes to be shunned." Mark Twain, Autobiography

"Complaining is an affirmation of life." Gilles Deleuze

"Making the private public, that's what poetry does." Allen Ginsberg

"There is nothing new in the world except the history you do not know." Harry S. Truman

This second volume of memoirs picks up where my first volume, *Out of Hitler's Shadow: Childhood and Youth in Germany and the United States, 1935-1967,* left off, namely with my return to the United States with my wife Steffi and my daughter Trina from five years of expatriation in Germany in the "drop-out" years of the 1960s. I taught high school English and social studies in Northeastern Vermont from 1967 to 1969, followed by a Ford Foundation Leadership Development Fellowship in 1970, and the resumption of my graduate education at the Universities of Vermont and Massachusetts, Amherst, where I earned a PhD in modern European history in 1974, a full eighteen years after my BA at Harvard in 1956. It was not a good time to enter the academic job market, as indeed I had been duly forewarned by my instructors as early as 1970. Several chapters in this book deal with the trials and tribulations of job-hunting in the unfavorable academic employment climate of the 1970s. I was very fortunate to have landed a tenure-track position at Gonzaga University in Spokane, Washington in 1978. Although I faced unexpected opposition from some members of my department, my application for tenure was eventually approved in 1982. I taught in the history department at Gonzaga until my retirement in 2004. The present volume covers the years from 1967 to 1982. If I live long enough and retain my mental functions, a third and final volume will follow.

After reading my first volume of memoirs, my good friend, the physician Peter Groza, whose grandfather Petru Groza (1884-1958) was the prime minister and later president of Romania from 1945 to 1958, asked me what I was trying to accomplish. Was there a message I was trying to get across, and if so, what was it? It was a good question to which I had no ready answer. Of course, it was easy enough to explain that this was the story of my life from my unapologetically self-centered perspective. But why, and for what purpose? Aware that my unexceptional professional achievements hardly warranted a biography, I rationalized my efforts as a service to future generations of descendants who might be interested in how their ancestors and predecessors lived and reacted to the events and conditions of our benighted age. But if I am completely honest—and honesty is the indispensible feature of any autobiography worth reading—I have to admit that I undertook this project with greater ambitions than simply leaving a record of my brief time on earth. I wanted to create, if not a work of literature, at least an aesthetically structured and enjoyably readable representation of my past that might give my otherwise rather insignificant existence some coherence and perhaps even meaning. My inspiration here was Alexander Nehemas' provocative intellectual biography of Nietzsche, *Life as Literature* (1985), which I reviewed for *German Studies Review* in 1988. Fashioning one's experiences and actions into a coherent account of one's life is "to become who one is." As in my first volume of memoirs, I have consulted and relied on personal journals I have kept intermittently all my life. The very act of reconstructing my past, based not only on fallible memory but on documentary evidence as well, has been its own reward.

Some members of my immediate and extended families who have followed this narrative on my blog have criticized my method as too personal. That is not surprising, as it has been my intention from the start to put as much as I could of my most subjective inner self into what I write in this, the end stage of my life. Unlike Mama, who in her eighties famously compared putting her memories on tape and being interviewed about her life to "running naked through Grand Central Station," I have no similar inhibitions. Indeed I positively enjoy this opportunity to exhibit my biases and vent my opinions, especially on political issues. So if I am accused of being [too] self-absorbed and self-involved, my critics are absolutely right. This particular *apologia pro vita sua* is served up entirely unapologetically. No one is obliged to read what I write, but whether they read or not, I will continue to write. If anyone objects that I am just writing for myself, my response is, so be it.

Again, as acknowledged in the preface to my first volume, my greatest debt is to my wife Sally and my son Emmet who have supported my rather eccentric exercise in intro- and retrospection throughout, even when, as has often been the case, they have disagreed with my conclusions or even with my premises, and most particularly with my judgments as to what to include in or exclude from the story of my life. While they didn't object to my disclosing the skeletons in my own closet, they disputed my right to air the dirty laundry of my siblings or close relatives. A totally unexpurgated version of my journals will have to await my death. Without questioning my veracity or sincerity, Sally has frequently reminded me that autobiography is perforce only one perspective on events that could easily be seen and portrayed very differently by other participants or witnesses, including the family members discussed or mentioned in my book. I have derived pleasure and strength from the memoirs of many other writers, some well-known ones such as Nietzsche's magnificent *Ecce Homo*, others quite obscure. If only a single reader, perhaps a generation or two hence, derives pleasure or strength from what I have written, my purpose will have been served.

I
The Irasburg Affair, 1967-1968

Steffi, the baby Trina, and I docked in New York on July 1st, 1967, almost exactly 21 years after my first arrival in New York as an eleven-year old after the war. Another new beginning for me, now aged 32 with a German wife, a one-year-old daughter, and badly frayed literary ambitions. At times it seemed to me I was repeating as farce what Mama had experienced as tragedy! Unconsciously I had heeded Pete Seeger's call, "The time for exiles is over." I got a far warmer dockside reception from my family than I expected – or probably deserved. Mama met us at the boat as promised, as did Olaf and Tempy, who was now working for a brokerage firm on Wall Street. Olaf drove us to Vermont in his VW bus, stopping for the night in Middletown, Connecticut, where he was teaching in the summer session at Wesleyan University. Driving by a power plant near Hartford, I could not help but think of similar installations that were—perhaps at that very moment—the targets of American bombs in Vietnam. The war hung like an invisible shroud over everything I saw, giving all the familiar scenes a peculiar unreality, as if normalcy were merely being faked.

And yet the summer of 1967 lingers in my memory as the most idyllic summer of my life. Mama's ramshackle, hand-built hut had few comforts (one of them being a toilet that could be flushed with a pail of water), but it was cozy and snug. Situated on 150 acres of rolling farmland, surrounded by forested hills, and with no other human habitation within our range of vision (Connie's farm, where Mama now resided, was just beyond the horizon), Mama's place perfectly embodied Vermont's lush green beauty and stark natural solitude. Sunrise in Albany, Vermont in July 1967 was as close

1

to Paradise—or at least its earthly representation—as I have come in my life. We had great luck with the weather: July and August were clear, sunny, and warm. The landscape and the climate formed the perfect backdrop for the honeymoon we never had. In San Francisco they were celebrating the "summer of love." Steffi and I had our own summer of love in rural Vermont.

We also had more than our share of good luck in finding a three-story, four-bedroom farmhouse on the common in the center of the neighboring village of Irasburg for sale for only $6,000. Having squirreled away 6,000 DM in our savings account in Berlin, just enough to convert into a 25 percent $1,500 down payment, we could actually afford to buy.

Our farmhouse on the common in Irasburg

Remarkably, the house came fully furnished as well. Its owner, Annie Mae Fisher, in her early 80s and immobilized by arthritis, lived in an adult-care home in the nearby village of Barton. With no living heirs, she had turned over responsibility for the upkeep and eventual sale of the property to Homer Sheltra, who had run the Irasburg general store for decades, but had recently undergone a laryngectomy for cancer and was anxious to leave for his new home in Connecticut as soon as possible. His health failing, he did not want to go through the trouble of organizing an estate sale. We were the beneficiaries of his impatience. We also benefitted from the prevailing disdain for "old junk." Natives of this isolated corner of Vermont were just beginning to understand the potential value of antiques.

Irasburg across the common, looking toward the southeast

We paid a visit to Annie Mae Fisher in Barton, determined as we were to maintain the home in the spirit of her family's long tradition in Irasburg. The house was built in 1881 with Victorian dimensions (though without most of the frills of that architectural style) after the original house on that site had burned down. Her father had lived in Irasburg since returning from the Civil War in 1865, in which he had been severely wounded. Besides the farm he ran a livery stable as well. Annie was completely under his spell.

"I had the most wonderful father there ever was."

She told us about a man she had met in an ice cream parlor at York Beach in Maine, where she had worked summers as a young woman. When he wrote her and asked if he might visit her in Irasburg, her mother did not give her permission. Her father said, "Well, Nannie, you've got to ask yourself whether you want to marry him." Annie said, he hadn't asked her, but she wrote him and told him not to come. Twenty years later she read in the *Boston Post* that he had become Boston police chief and was happily married with two children. She rushed home and showed her father the clipping. "See what I might have been?"— "Well, Annie, I hope I didn't keep you from getting a husband." But Annie told him she had no regrets. She had preferred to make her father a good home. "They say opportunity comes only once in a lifetime. I think our lives are predestined, don't you? It's all governed by fate."

The barn had collapsed some years ago under the weight of a Vermont winter snowfall, but the house was structurally sound. It needed only cosmetic work, most of which we were able to do ourselves. After weeks of painting, laying tile, repairing, and cleaning, we finally moved in just before the beginning of the school year in September. Heat was the major problem we had to confront that first year. The wood-burning furnace in the cellar was beyond repair. We were forced to rely on a centrally located pot-bellied stove and a wood-burning kitchen range. It was not until the following year that we could afford to install an oil-burning central heating system (which since has been replaced by another wood-burning furnace). We got some indication of what we could expect from a Vermont winter when returning from a day trip to Expo 67 in Montreal at the beginning of October we found that the temperature had already dipped well below freezing at dusk. Our babysitter, Paulette Beaudry, had been forced to take refuge with Trina in her own heated home across the common.

Steffi in her workshop in Irasburg, ca. 1969

Teaching high school in northern Vermont required some adjustment on my part. Although the dairy-farming economy was in severe decline in Orleans County, much of the local farming population still regarded secondary schooling as unwelcome competition for the time and services of the young people whose labor was needed on the farms. Having had little experience with reluctant students, I had to adjust to the unanticipated reality that many of my students simply regarded school as a waste of time. I thought I could use the techniques I learned in the army to enforce discipline, but soon realized my mistake. Military-style threats and commands just provoked laughter and scorn. I had no trouble controlling my own classes, where I knew that the secret of success was to keep students busy. Most of my preparatory time was spent devising interesting assignments, exercises, and activities. The more difficult challenge was to enforce silence in the school library, which served as the "study hall" for students between classes. Teachers took turns in monitoring the study hall. I finally decided to allow talking as long as it was not disruptive. This was not a decision with which everyone agreed. How best to cope with potential insubordination was the main topic of discussion at the first few faculty meetings of the year. Some older members of the faculty, in particular, viewed relations between students and teachers as inherently antagonistic. To them nothing less than control of the new school was at stake in the fall of 1967. The former principal of Orleans High School, now in his sixties and still smarting from having been passed over as principal of the new Lake Region Union High School, advocated imposing one-way traffic on the stairways as a way to regiment the student body. He warned that any relaxation of discipline or concession to student autonomy would only encourage rebellion. Another older faculty member complained, "What I don't like is that long hair and those mustaches that some of them are growing." Even one or two of the younger faculty members were scornful of my permissive attitude. "You just want to be liked. You're not tough enough. This morning I found 'SHAW SUCKS' written across the board. That shows I'm getting somewhere." However, under the leadership of our new principal Millard Harrison, still in his thirties, less confrontational attitudes and practices prevailed. The times they were a-changing, to my great delight. In my journal I noted that

discussion with [math teacher] Fred May on enforcement of a code on dress and grooming got stuck when I could not "draw the line" between

5

permissible and impermissible. Now I can: the line is each individual's sense of shame or embarrassment (insofar as health standards can't be invoked, or standards of "public disturbance.")

Weighing on everyone's mind was the Vietnam War. Increasingly one could feel that opinion on the war was shifting. Some of our younger faculty members had gone into teaching to gain deferment from the draft, greatly adding, in most cases, to the quality of instruction. Most young people, whether liable to the draft or not, were overwhelmingly critical of the war. It was a relief not to have to hide my own thoughts and feelings for fear of social opprobrium. At first I was reluctant to openly express my opposition to the war for fear of antagonizing my colleagues and jeopardizing my job. I soon discovered, however, that my colleagues, not knowing where I stood, were equally wary about freely expressing their anti-war opinions to me! Most took refuge in a non-committal avowal of the magnitude of the problem and the absence of any easy solution. At lunch in the faculty dining room in September 1967 our dynamic music and band teacher Chuck Milazzo empathized with the quandary in which President Johnson found himself: "What can he do?" Chuck asked, rhetorically. "He can stop making war," I said. It may have been the stark simplicity of this proposal that stunned everyone into silence, but I interpreted it as a sign of agreement. In my homeroom I tacked up an over-sized placard Steffi had drawn for me on the theme of "make love, not war." Word got around, and students, faculty, and even administrators stopped by to admire it. Nobody asked me to take it down.

Not surprisingly, my best friends among the faculty were also the strongest opponents of the war. Young David LaRoche, a tough and brawny former football player at Boston University now teaching social studies at Lake Region, made me feel almost "moderate" by comparison, although I shared his hope that the Viet Cong would not cave in to the fearsome firepower of the American military. "I hope the North Vietnamese don't back down," David said. "I hope they'll stand firm. It would be a blow to all of us if they didn't." We understood that there was much more at stake in this war than merely control of South Vietnam. More important in the long run was the domestic conflict between the "hawks" and the" doves," the "right" and the "left," the "cold warriors" and the "peaceniks," the "establishment" and the "counter-culture," two schools of thought with very different conceptions of American interests and the policies needed to achieve them. My journal entries give some indication of the centrality of the war in our thoughts and the bitterness of the debate it generated.

Sep. 10, 1967 The matter-of-factness with which deaths in Viet Nam are accepted (except insofar as they represent signs of weakness or loss in battle) makes me no longer wonder how, for a number of years, people [in Nazi Germany] could proudly publish: *"Gefallen für Führer, Volk und Vaterland."*

The archbishop of San Antonio says force is necessary in the world because of the existence of evil. Another proof, as if any more were needed, that it is the "good" and the "just" from whom the greatest danger emanates (because they will always have the most power). Why does it never occur to them that the evil, the existence of which they are so sure of, may just as well be lodged in themselves?

Oct. 15 Rusk on Vietnam: "Now let's not be children." This is the argument against the hippies, artists—everything that challenges the artifact. What he means is, "Now let's not bring morality into this. Let's be grown-up and regard the war as merely a geopolitical problem."

The *New York Times*: Rusk appealing to fear in the masses: "Escalation of American involvement that now induces the administration to evoke objectives that will appear large enough to justify a half-million American troops ..."

The bad conscience behind our intervention in Vietnam—the feeling of needing an enemy—of deserving an enemy.

Nov. 14 Vietnam makes everything everywhere seem immoral: every activity that is not concerned with Vietnam seems deliberately and perversely indifferent to it—amoral, leaving a worse taste than the actively immoral, the military, for instance...

Nov. 30 An interesting aspect of "limited" war: perhaps it is a partial admission that the degree of right in the war is also limited: the U.S.

does not feel right enough to use all its power. Each side is not only battling the other, but fighting for a share of right, which, paradoxically, can only be maintained by being on the defensive (both militarily and psychologically).

The respect for the enemy implicit in Mama's hawkish attitude: war is a part of life; do it well.

Mama's attitude on Vietnam is a concession of gratitude and loyalty to Vermont.

Dec. 4 The Vietnam War offers the same sort of false relief [of the body-politic] as blood-letting in the medical treatment of the last century: It crystallizes the general malaise and it mobilizes the body's forces against a specific injury.

Dec. 10 Why [W. H.] Auden and aware persons of that sort are not vehemently opposed to the Vietnam War (why Wordsworth turned conservative): The same thing that makes us oppose the war-makers—the feeling that the "establishment" is not checking its conduct through conscience—makes them oppose us. They recognize and distrust our motives just as much as we do theirs: they carry our feeling a step further—they recognize that we are even more destructive by nature, even more immodest in our aims...

Dec.16 The Vietnam War will change the meaning of the word "pacification" to include the idea of force.

Dec. 19 The Vietnam War: like a general inflammation that has finally come out in a boil. The pus is dripping out. In that sense I greet it: we will have a period of relative health thereafter.

Dec. 20 Three-quarters of Americans believe anti-war demonstrations "encourage Communists to fight all the harder": and what effect does the fact of their believing this (or saying that they do) have on the Communists?

Dec. 22 "More is at stake in Vietnam than just the 15 million people [of South Vietnam]," say the Asian scholars (Reischauer, et al.), perfectly willing to sacrifice these 15 million to their higher stakes.

Jan. 6, 1968 Question for a news conference: "What would you do, Mr. President, if you were head of the North Vietnamese state?"

Jan. 12 One good thing about a situation like Vietnam: it exposes people. They have got to show their true colors. Bob Hope and John Steinbeck get "burned off" about the guys who are always "anti." You don't hear so much about "destructive criticism" anymore, though; the irony would be too apparent.

Feb. 3 I know when they are shooting the Viet Cong, in their hearts they are shooting me and my kind. But in one sense the U.S. involvement will bear long-range fruit: it will legitimize Vietnamese independence and their regime, whatever form it takes. Both [independence and form of government] will be well-deserved and hard-earned. It would almost have been unfair of the U.S. not to remain true to historical laws and give Vietnamese national history this tremendous challenge. A quote at the right time (Dr. Johnson, quoted by W. H. Auden in the N.Y. Times): "I am afraid there is no other way of ascertaining the truth than by persecution on the one hand and enduring it on the other."

Feb. 24 In a sense, of course, the hawks are right: they must lash out and fight to survive: to retain their independence: they are too susceptible to the temptations of power to ever maintain their integrity if they do not have a hard-and-fast enemy to keep them on an even keel.

Feb. 27 Trying to understand the superior wisdom of people like Auden (supposedly backing the U.S. in Vietnam) or Mama: the great strength and relief in thinking that perhaps they see the tragedy of the U.S—some historical determinism that the strong must always test the young—and the stronger they are, the more they help them...

Mar. 9 Correspondence with Olaf: feeling I am doing him a favor by not mentioning Vietnam: yet angry that he should fail to acknowledge the favor by not mentioning Vietnam in his reply!

Behavior that we would consider neurotic in an individual is considered normal in a nation: boasting, rivalry, paranoia, hatred, abuse...

Why the Vietnam War is an effective "Rorschach Test": because it does take a certain instinct, a certain "awareness," a certain emotional reaction to "pick the right answers." "Reason" alone won't necessarily do it.

Mar. 14 It is eerie to think that the 20-year period between major wars had just about elapsed when the United States started bombing North Vietnam (1965). And it is even eerier to think that the only war the U.S. has a chance of winning is a world war (total war).

Mar. 15 By acting on the assumption of the Domino Theory, you make it a reality.

Mar. 23 Rusk: "I leave moral judgments to providence." The "humility" of not making moral judgments—of being immoral...

Mar. 26 On Vietnam: don't feel like a saint for quitting, feel like a criminal who's been released and cannot make good his crime.

Apr. 7 Why is the United States so scared? Do they realize, perhaps instinctively, that they are a nation of potential collaborators? This is the price for elevating success to the primary value in life. They are scared of themselves, knowing they have no inner resistance.

Meanwhile, the Tet Offensive had come and gone in January 1968, and President Johnson, almost defeated by Gene McCarthy in the New Hampshire primary and now facing the challenge of Bobby Kennedy's candidacy as well, made his dramatic exit from the presidential race at the end of March. The moment was unforgettable: when I heard his announcement on the TV in the kitchen, it felt like a deliverance and a totally unexpected ratification of the justice of our cause. Little did I realize at the time that it was only the first act in a tragic year of political and ideological conflict that would result in the election of Richard Nixon and a prolongation of the war for another five years. Only weeks after Johnson's exhilarating renunciation, Martin Luther King was assassinated. In early June it was Bobby Kennedy's turn, prompting the following sour reflections in my journal on June 5th, 1968:

> The terrible thing about Bobby Kennedy's assassination: its use by the other side to advance their own objectives: Johnson appointing a commission to investigate and curb "violence in the streets" (like Tempy's corps citing Nietzsche in defense of the Mensur [ritualized duel]). Ed Sullivan's show was never so bad as the one commemorating R. Kennedy's death: they did not feel they needed to change the show in the least, except to leave out the comedy acts. This left the usual sentimental, unctuous, mawkish drivel on flag and bible that one can watch with detachment on the Sundays when it is not soiling the memory of Kennedy.

> This assassination hurt less than John Kennedy's because I did not expect Bobby Kennedy to get in. It was not the keen disappointment that John Kennedy's death was. The forces of the right were too entrenched; Bob Kennedy's failure (inevitable, to my way of thinking) was only rendered more noble, more dramatic, by his death. JFK's death paved the way to something worse; RFK's death, if his message is heeded, may pave the way to something better.

1968 is now mainly remembered as a year of rebellion and emancipation all over the world. It was the year of the Columbia University student uprising, of the May Revolt in France, and of the "Prague Spring," so cruelly crushed by the Soviet invasion of Czechoslovakia in August of that year. In this country the cultural revolution brought about by the confluence of the civil rights, anti-war, and feminist movements was in full swing. It was a year of continued urban disorders, student protests, and the Poor People's Campaign in Washington, DC. But in the end it was the forces backing "law and order" and a continuation of the war that won out. The incipient backlash against the protest movements of the left stands out as the most ominous development of that turbulent year. A highly polarized and violent electoral campaign culminated in the victory of Nixon's "silent majority." Vermont was by no means immune to the political and ideological conflict that racked the nation as a whole. In fact, in the summer of 1968 the tiny village of Irasburg was the site of a political "affair" that captured national attention and reflected in microcosm the political forces that were dividing the nation. Here is how I described the events of that summer in a thesis written for the MA degree in history at the University of Vermont in 1971:

"The people of the world could learn a lot from Irasburg," said Reverend David Lee Johnson, commenting on the warm welcome he received from neighbors and townspeople on his arrival from California. At the time he did not realize the irony this statement was later to acquire. Johnson, his wife, and four children had come to Vermont from Seaside, a city in California, which, despite its idyllic name, has a racially mixed population of approximately 25,000 and is beset by all the familiar problems of urbanization. Johnson had come to sparsely populated Irasburg in order to get away from racial conflict, only to find himself embroiled within a matter of weeks in a complex series of events that came euphemistically to be known as the Irasburg Affair.

These are the facts of the case as they appeared to the public: Johnson and his family arrived in Irasburg on July 4th, 1968, the first African-American family to have taken up residence there within living memory. They were accompanied by Mrs. Barbara Lawrence, a 23 year old white woman, and her two young children. Mrs. Lawrence, a next-door neighbor of the Johnsons in California, and her husband, who was serving in the army, had recently filed for divorce.

In the night of July 18 to 19, exactly two weeks after the Johnsons' arrival, a shotgun attack was made on the large, thirteen-room Victorian house on Route 14, just north of the village common into which the Johnson family had moved. The shots came from a late-model sedan, described by the Johnsons as red and white on top, as it proceeded by the house in a northerly direction. While the vehicle and its three passengers turned for a second foray, Johnson had time to fetch and load the revolver he had in his possession, and as the attackers passed the house again, this time heading south, Johnson returned fire. The vehicle disappeared into the night.

The attack had left several shattered window panes in the Johnson home, but aside from ruffled nerves none of the residents were injured. The state police, alerted by a call placed from a neighbor's home, arrived shortly thereafter. So did the press and the television crews, and the case received front page coverage in Vermont newspapers the following day, and for many days to come. Members of the community expressed outrage at the attack and extended their sympathy to the Johnsons. Reverend Roger Albright, Executive Minister of the Vermont Council of Churches, went on the air the following day with a panel of clergy and laymen. Another member of the panel was Reverend Gordon Newell, minister of the Cross Mountain Parish that includes the United Church of Christ in Irasburg. Over Radio WIKE in Newport they cautioned against vigilante activities and pointed out that Vermont was not isolated from the racial problems that beset the country at large. Reverend Newell said: "We will do everything we can to make the Johnsons feel a sense of dignity and a feeling of belonging. David tells me he's not going to leave and he won't let anyone run him out. We won't let anyone make him go, either."

Not all the voices raised were as conciliatory as this one. Emory Hebard of Glover, Chairman of the Vermont House Ways and Means Committee and Republican representative for the district that includes Irasburg, used the incident for a political attack on Democratic Governor Philip H. Hoff. "The governor and his people are determined to stir up Vermont, and created problems, and certainly deserved this one." He felt that the unrest in Irasburg was a result of the Vermont-New York City Summer Youth Program, launched by Governor Hoff as a response to the racial crisis that gripped many of the nation's cities at the time. This program, designed to foster better racial understanding by enabling urban ghetto youths to spend a summer working with youths in Vermont, continued to arouse considerable popular hostility in Vermont throughout the summer of 1968.

Although Vermont Attorney General James L. Oakes underlined the importance he attached to the case by personally visiting the site of the attack in Irasburg, the state police appeared to make no immediate headway in their search for the culprits. Several days after the attack it became known that the police was conducting an inquiry into Johnson's background, presumably in search of a clue to the nightrider attack. On July 21 the 24-hour guard that was originally to have been maintained at the Johnson home until the case was broken, was called off on the grounds that, since the Johnson home now had a telephone, police could be summoned in case of trouble.

In the days that followed there were signs that relations between Johnson and the policemen assigned to the case were less than amiable. On July 28 Johnson requested Governor Hoff to remove Sgt. William Chilton from the case for an allegedly racist attitude. Sgt. Chilton had apparently indicated to Johnson that he had exercised poor judgment in returning fire on the attacking vehicle. Chilton felt that an ordained minister should have exhibited a more Christian attitude. According to Chilton, the "birdshot" used in the shot-gun attack was relatively harmless and there had been no intent to kill. On July 29 news reports indicated that no clue to the identity of the attackers had yet been uncovered. Rumors began to circulate that Johnson had staged the incident himself in order to reap the sympathy that would accrue to him as the victim of a racial attack. Hate mail and insulting phone calls increasingly replaced the expressions of sympathy and support that Johnson had originally received from throughout the state.

On July 31, the *Burlington Free Press* carried a front-page article under the headline, "Officials Say Irasburg Shooting Not a Hoax." In the same report Colonel Erwin A. Alexander, a native of Glover and as Commissioner of the Office of Public Safety the top police officer in the state, was quoted as saying, "If and when the case develops I think you will find three or four young fellows had a little beer and thought they would shake the minister up a little." Questioned about the investigation into Johnson's background, Alexander said, "When stories told by the Reverend Mr. Johnson don't add up, then they have to be checked."

On August 1 the papers reported that Attorney General Oakes was considering requesting Hoff to authorize a $1,000 reward for information leading to an arrest, but this was no longer necessary. On that same date, fourteen days after the night of the attack, 21-year-old Larry Conley of Glover was arrested for the crime and charged with a breach of peace. In a departure from usual practice, Col. Alexander accompanied the arrest with a statement to the public: "The case has no racial overtones and was not caused by racial prejudice. Today's events did much to remove a stigma unfairly attached to the State of Vermont as a whole and the Northeast Kingdom in particular."

Larry Conley, an army sergeant home on leave, was the son of businessman Howard Conley, a man of some wealth and influence in the area. His numerous business interests included a fence factory, a store, two car dealerships and a sawmill; he also served as Chairman of the Orleans Central School District. Conley reacted vehemently to his son's arrest: "They've been hunting my boy since he got home on furlough. Talk about discrimination." His charge that Johnson was being accorded preferential treatment on account of his race was to be heard recurrently in the weeks to come. Although Larry Conley pleaded not guilty at first, in the face of an incriminating statement by Richard LeClair, the driver of the attacking vehicle on the night of the shooting, he subsequently changed his plea to *nolo contendere*. On August 22 he received a suspended sentence of six to eighteen months and was fined $500, but by this time public interest focused sharply on a new set of events.

On August 9, five days before Larry Conley was originally scheduled to go on trial, Johnson had again made front page headlines. He and Barbara Lawrence were arrested at gunpoint in Bethel, Vermont, while apparently on their way to Fort Devens, Massachusetts, from where Mrs. Lawrence had planned to return to California. They were taken to Newport and booked on a charge of adultery. State Trooper Jean Lessard, assigned to guard duty at the Johnson home had discovered Johnson and Mrs. Lawrence in the act of sexual intercourse on the living room sofa at 5:30 in the morning on July 22, three days after the shooting. (At the board of inquiry hearings in November Lessard testified that he had not actually seen the act of intercourse, but had concluded that it had taken place or was about to take place.) Lessard said he had entered the room to get a cup of coffee. After several hours of questioning by police in the Derby substation, Mrs. Lawrence had signed a statement on July 26 admitting to sexual relations with Rev. Johnson. In a second statement eleven days later she denied her previous confession and contended she had signed it under police pressure. (A third signed statement, confirming the authenticity of her signature on the first one but refusing to reaffirm or deny the confession was introduced by police at the board of inquiry hearings in November.) On August 12 Mrs. Lawrence pleaded *nolo contendere* to the charge of adultery in the Orleans District Court in Newport, and Judge Lewis Springer gave her a suspended sentence of six to twelve months, imposed a fine of $125 and court costs, and instructed her to have no further communication with Rev. Johnson. Mrs. Lawrence subsequently returned to California.

Johnson himself proved less easy to convict. He stuck by his plea of not guilty and through his attorney Robert D. Rachlin of St. Johnsbury entered a motion for a change of venue on the grounds of racial discrimination in Orleans County. Although Judge Springer found that the police officer in charge of the district, Lt. Clement Potvin, had exhibited racial bias in some of his utterances, he denied the change of venue and set the date of trial for the second week in September. It was, however never to take place. Having requested and failed to receive legal support from the attorney general's office in Montpelier, Orleans County State's Attorney Leonard Pearson, who had signed the warrant for Johnson's arrest, found that he could not successfully prosecute the case. Attorney General Oakes refused his assistance on the grounds that prosecution in such cases was not customary when no complaint had been filed by "an aggrieved spouse." A trip to California (costing the state in excess of $1,000) by Detective Laurence Wade and, for reasons never explained, Orange County State's Attorney Philip Angell, Jr., failed to obtain Mrs. Lawrence's return to Vermont where her testimony was vital for a jury-tight case against Johnson. Nor did the *Burlington Free Press*, whose assistance in checking Johnson's background had been enlisted by the police, succeed in turning up useful evidence, though on September 29 blazing headlines in the *Vermont Sunday News* announced that Johnson had been convicted for a misdemeanor (carrying a concealed weapon) in Florida in 1952. When the state's attorney dropped his case against Johnson on September 11, the suspicion of moral blemish remained.

Meanwhile the climate of harassment and intimidation reached a high pitch on Labor Day, September 3, when six men were arrested for threatening and verbally abusing Johnson in two separate incidents. Four of these men pleaded guilty to a breach of peace and were given suspended thirty-day sentences and fined $25 apiece on October 16. The two others, arraigned by Deputy Attorney General Frank Mahady on September 13 when it became apparent that State's Attorney Pearson was planning no action against them, held out for a jury trial. After Feliciano Vigario of Barton was acquitted by a jury on November 1, charges against Patrick McMahon of Orleans were dropped.

On September 11 Governor Hoff had announced that he would appoint a board of inquiry to investigate the circumstances surrounding what was by now generally referred to as the Irasburg Affair: "I think the people of Vermont are entitled to know what this is all about." U.S. Judge Ernest W. Gibson, who as former governor had been instrumental in establishing the state police organization in 1947, headed a three-man board, which also included attorney Hilton H. Wick of Burlington and Dorothy Collins of Hyde Park, former president of Vermont College in Montpelier.

After the hearings of the board (held in Newport on November 7 and 8 and in Montpelier on November 15, 16, and 22 of that year), what had long been suspected by some persons became public knowledge: police conduct of the case had been, in the words of the board, "unusual". Among the instances of negligence uncovered by the board was the revelation that Larry Conley had been a prime suspect within 24 hours after the shooting attack. At 10:30 on the morning after the attack Lt. Potvin was informed by Bruce Brown in Rev. Newell's residence that Larry Conley was among the persons involved in the attack. In his report Detective Wade stated that by 11:00 p.m. on July 19, less than 24 hours after the shooting, Larry Conley was a prime suspect. By the evening of July 21 Conley's alibi was shattered through interviews with the two persons Conley claimed to have seen in Jay's snack bar in Derby at the time of the attack. The board concluded that none of this information was relayed to Attorney General Oakes until July 25, and then only in incomplete form. Action toward Conley's arrest was taken only after Oakes had assigned Deputy Attorney General Mahady and Investigator Gregory L'Ecuyer to the case with instructions to stay on it until it was solved. They, too, were hampered by the failure of police investigators to communicate their findings to them. It was not until July 30 that they learned of the hole in Conley's alibi. On July 31, after being questioned by Potvin, Mahady, and L'Ecuyer, Richard LeClair, the driver of the car from which Conley shot at the Johnson home, offered to testify for the state if he were granted immunity from prosecution. The following day Conley was arrested on a warrant made out by Mahady, which State's Attorney Pearson refused to sign.

The board concluded that Conley "might never have been convicted of the shooting episode had it not been for the activity of the attorney general's office." The board also criticized the police for launching an investigation into Johnson's background on July 21, a day before the alleged adulterous act took place. No equivalent background investigation was ever made of the prime suspect in the case, Larry Conley, although such an investigation would have revealed at least one previous involvement in a racial incident. On July 13, less than a week before the shooting incident, he had verbally molested a group of African-American participants in the New York-Vermont Youth Project at the Barton State Park. The board emphasized that, contrary to the statement issued by Commissioner Alexander, racial prejudice had indeed been involved in the shooting episode. In its most widely publicized conclusion the board insisted that the issue was not Mr. Johnson's moral character, but rather the safety of a man's home in Vermont.

It would seem that the findings of the Gibson Commission had clarified the controversy once and for all, but in fact they served only to draw the partisan lines more firmly. Governor Hoff's efforts to implement some of the board's recommendations were successfully resisted by Commissioner Alexander. On December 20 Hoff had formally censured Alexander for prejudging the presence or absence of racial prejudice in a pending court case, failing to cooperate with the attorney general's office, and leaking information to various newspapers. He requested that by January 2 Alexander submit plans for disciplinary action against three of the police officers whose conduct had been singled out for specific criticism by the board. Hoff also asked Alexander to explain the organization within the police force itself to which some of the testimony presented to the board had pointed, and to supply "detailed and specific plans as to what steps [he] and the department will take to see to it that no similar omissions or actions will occur in the future." Claiming he needed a full transcript of the board hearings in order to determine the extent of wrongdoing, Alexander stalled with the apparent intention of waiting for Hoff's departure from office on January 9, 1969, and the accession of Republican Deane C. Davis to the governor's seat. Although Hoff again censured Alexander for defiance, he did not have the heart to fire a man with forty years' experience.

When Alexander told the press, "There is such a thing as beating a dead horse too much," he was expressing a line of argument now increasingly to be heard from opponents of the board. Even before the board had first convened, the *Newport Daily Express* had referred to the Irasburg Affair as a "closed case." Now that the adultery charge against Johnson had been dropped, anyone referring derogatorily to the handling of the affair was cast in the role of deliberate trouble-maker. State Senator-elect Fred Westphal, a Republican representing Orleans County in the House at the time, led the public opposition to Hoff's actions and called for a joint House-Senate subcommittee with subpoena powers to investigate the board of inquiry itself. Robert Eldredge of Montpelier, attorney for Alexander, told newsmen that "this investigation has hurt Vermont unjustly and unfairly."

In an editorial casting aspersions on Johnson's moral character, the *Newport Daily Express* had previously implied that Johnson had been sent to Irasburg by outside interests in order to gain a foothold for Negro settlement in this part of the country. This suggestion of conspiracy was heard again after *Life Magazine*, with its keen nose for readable copy, published a fair, if somewhat flippant, account of the Irasburg Affair in its issue of April 4, 1969. Again the *Newport Daily Express* responded with an editorial admonishing those who would reopen the case, while at the same time asserting that the full story behind the affair was not yet known.

Meanwhile Governor Davis had released Commissioner Alexander of the obligation to take disciplinary action in the case. Alexander had continued to deny that the transcript of testimony presented at the board hearings justified such action. In a letter to Governor Davis he said the officers in question had conducted themselves in a highly professional manner. He accused the press of inaccurate coverage, the clergy of unwarranted interference, and Johnson and his family of "irresponsible and erratic behavior." His greatest fire was reserved for former Attorney General Oakes, whose opinions, as expressed to the board, resulted, according to Alexander, "from inexperience in the field of investigation or were formulated for some reason unknown to this officer."

In the more conservative ideological climate of the Davis administration Alexander's defiance of the board was no longer viewed as insubordination. In the same letter in which he informed Commissioner Alexander that he would not require disciplinary action, Governor Davis instructed the Commissioner to establish a state police policy under which good law enforcement is accomplished with equal impartiality to all and to establish procedures to insure full communication, cooperation, and exchange of information between the Public Safety Department and the attorney general's office. At the same time Davis made it clear that he was closing the case: "I feel very strongly the time has come to bring this controversy to an end." Commissioner Alexander secured early retirement on October 1, 1969.

Johnson himself, embittered and obliged to seek employment elsewhere, recalled his family to California in January 1969. ... The historian, who must see the attack in the context of long-term events, cannot fail but note that in the last analysis the night-riders achieved the apparent objective of their attack: to persuade the Johnsons to leave. It is a bitterly ironical aspect of the case that this objective was finally achieved with official sanction, indeed with official support...

The Irasburg Affair was a microcosm of the "racial problem" (in practice, the exclusion and repression of Negroes) in America. Viewed in a larger context it was neither unique nor isolated. Neither its location nor its timing were entirely fortuitous. It did not have to happen, but it is no accident that it happened where it did, how it did, and even when it did. It was part of a white backlash that manifested itself, to a greater or lesser degree, across the nation in the latter part of 1968. Racism, of course, has a far longer history than this. But there is some reason to believe, in the case of David Johnson, that the worst effects of generalized racial prejudice in the population at large could have been overcome in time if community leaders had recognized the importance of this goal and had lent their support to its achievement. They did not do so primarily because Johnson was perceived as a threatening representative of the Black movement for equal rights that marked early and middle years of the decade. Precisely because he was perceived as the threatening vanguard of a black mass movement, the full force of conservative opinion was turned against a single family. It is likely that Representative Emory Hebard expressed the feelings of many influential members of the community when he said, "If the Johnson family have come to Vermont to be ordinary law-abiding citizens, I am pleased they are here, but if their purpose is to put Orleans County through a travail of civil rights, I just as soon they hadn't come."

The police reflected and contributed to the dominant sentiment in the community. In the minds of its leadership the police had done no wrong because it had simply defended the community and its moral standards against a perceived threat from outside. Again the conclusion suggests itself that individual racial prejudice within the police force, pernicious though it may be in its consequences, is not the paramount problem (and in any case is not easily amenable to change.) The paramount problem (and one that can more readily be dealt with) was the politicization of the police, the emergence of the police as an ideological force in the political arena and as an independent body answerable only to itself. Racial attitudes influence the functioning of institutions and these in turn nurture prejudice. But the institutions do the real damage; efforts to break the vicious circularity of prejudice and to insure racial and social justice should be aimed at reforming these.

A precondition of more equitable law enforcement—if the Irasburg Affair is any guide—is greater public sensitivity to the discretionary role of the police in matters of law enforcement. The central problem in the Irasburg Affair appeared to be the propensity of the police to apply the law in accordance with its ideological preferences. Technically the police always has a rationalization to act: for that reason it is important to recognize the ideological motivation behind police actions. This, in turn, is only possible if police practices are to some degree or in some way visible to the public.

The Irasburg Affair gave further evidence, if any were needed, that attitudes favoring racial inequality are not an exclusively Southern problem. In the North, more so, it would seem, than in the South, there is an additional factor, very clearly manifest in the Irasburg Affair: the widespread unwillingness to admit the existence of such attitudes. The most intractable problems are those rendered invisible and inaccessible by hypocrisy. A prerequisite to their solution is to bring them out into the open. This is part of the historian's task. Insofar as hypocrisy about racial prejudice reflects at least an ideal of racial equality, there is hope that an awareness of the disparity between ideal and practice can lead to a rectification of inequality.

On the basis of the Irasburg Affair one is tempted to conclude that if our institutions function according to the values that we, as a nation, profess (and effective leadership is vital to such institutional functioning), the more pernicious effects of racism can at least be kept under control. One of the most heartening aspects of the case was the willingness of top state officials, specifically Hoff and Oakes, to risk political disadvantage for the sake of justice. Both his supporters and his opponents felt that Oakes' part in the case contributed, perhaps decisively, to his defeat in the Republican primary for Governor on September 9, 1968. Critics of Oakes' role in the Johnson case, such as the *Burlington Free Press*, gave their wholehearted support to Dean Davis, a representative of the state's traditionally conservative point of view. A less courageous man in the governor's office than Philip Hoff would hardly have appointed an investigative commission, without which the extent of police culpability would undoubtedly never have been revealed. The Irasburg Affair would have gone down on record as just another case in which a trouble-prone Negro ran afoul of the law. Just how much Hoff's role in this case contributed to his defeat in the 1970 senatorial election is hard to determine, but the race issue surfaced explosively when cartoonist Al Capp, speaking at a Republican dinner, accused Hoff of wanting to bring rapists into Vermont.

Yet despite the courage of Hoff and Oakes, the fact remains that the board itself had no powers of subpoena or enforcement, and that no action was ever taken to implement its recommendations, much less to prosecute the misconduct revealed by the board. In this sense the board shared the fate of a number of commissions on a national level in recent years. Its effectiveness was contingent on the degree to which the information it revealed would serve an educational purpose. In view of the hostility with which the board was regarded even before its findings were released, it is questionable whether its message ever reached the audience for which it was meant. Nevertheless, Judge Gibson was optimistic that in this respect, at least, the investigation had fulfilled its function well: "It's making people think twice about it. I think it's a very good thing in the long run." Attorney Hilton Wick concurred: "We're more mindful now of the problem."

The Irasburg Affair as a therapeutic crisis: this is perhaps the most comforting conclusion we can draw. For the Johnsons, to be sure, the Irasburg Affair was an experience of the kind to which Negroes in America have had to grow accustomed—another case of "justice delayed and hope deferred."

How the times have changed! In those days I could never have imagined that Vermont was destined to become one of the most staunchly progressive states in the nation and that in 2008 an African American would be elected President of the United States. On July 30, 1968, I recorded my first comment in my journal on the nightrider attack on the Johnson family and the gradual shift of public opinion from

> Indignation to indifference to doubt. State police: the house will be guarded until the case is solved (my reaction to first hearing this on TV: what if it is never solved? This turns out to be the case.) Talk of the town is, he did it himself. In their exasperation at not being able to find the attackers, the police seem to be turning to this view, too. Newspaper report: "The thrust of the investigation has been into Mr. Johnson's background." Asking to see marriage license. "Why do you have new cars? Why did you shoot back?" Doubt becoming the form and substance of racial prejudice. Fighting the feeling in myself. Wishing to hell he were a more clear-cut case of good vs. evil. Blaming him mentally for giving his "foes" such good arguments.
>
> Irony: The ones who fired the shotgun will have accomplished their purpose. Johnson will be forced to leave—despite his heart-warming pledge that first night on TV, "I won't run" (the landlady won't rent and he can't get the loan to buy. The real culprits: the property owners, the employers, not the hoods with the shotgun.)
>
> And through all of this the feeling that I can't help but seem patronizing, because I don't have his problems and can't solve them. The fact that many white people find me condescending as well plays a part in my self-reproach. Feelings of guilt are compounded by Johnson's plans to leave. Where to?—"Not Irasburg."

I did not believe Johnson when he said that the state police was not making a maximum effort to catch the culprits, but of course he turned out to be right. My inability to recognize or affirm the existence of racism within the police: was that itself a deeply ingrained form of racism? After Johnson's arrest on a charge of adultery on August 9th it finally became clear even to me that racism was at the root of police conduct in the case. I wrote a letter to the editor of the *Burlington Free Press* to expressing my exasperation and disgust.

This case has provided textbook examples of every form of racial persecution. Now even the authorities seem bent on illustrating what up to now one was tempted to dismiss as a black militant cliché: the white man's fear of the black man's sexuality.

How bitterly ironical that the shots fired by nightriders four weeks ago should now achieve their desired objective with official approval!

I was painfully aware that a letter to the editor could also serve as a device to sooth one's conscience for not giving any concrete financial help, which I was in no position—and frankly unwilling—to provide. My relations with Johnson were never close enough for true friendship. I found his attitudes irritatingly conventional: he was hawkish about Vietnam, critical of radicals, and insisted on being called a Negro rather than a Black man. He disagreed with me when I said that the issue was not whether he had committed adultery, but rather the questionable validity of so antiquated and repressive a law and its highly discretionary enforcement against Johnson. Whether he was "guilty" of this so-called crime was irrelevant to me. "No," he said, "I'd accept my punishment if I were guilty, but I'm innocent. Why should I swing if I'm innocent?" When I invited him to a cook-out at our home, he pointed to a barn in the distance and asked, "How many acres is all the land you can see from that barn to here?"—"Oh, at least 500 acres, I'd say."—"That's how much I'd like to own." He was implicitly critical of the hamburgers and hot dogs we served. "After we get settled in you'll have to come over to our place for a real cookout, barbecued steaks and so on."

His seventeen-year-old son George was less materialistic and more militant. While his father sought only to join the property-owning middle class and get his share of the pie, his son seemed more sensitive to blows to his ethnic and family pride. Ironically, community resentment was concentrated against the father, who posed the more immediate threat to white hegemony. The relationship between father and son mirrored in microcosm the generational revolt that was taking place on a national scale. I had a chance to experience this generational conflict as well when George joined my senior English class at Lake Region in the fall of 1968.

How George's presence in class has served to point up the flaws or superficiality in almost everything we've read. Every time I pick a book for the class I think, "this one at least can't be offensive." And yet it turns out that it is. The most offensive one was the Conrad Richter short story on the savage Indians, with "black" used on at least four occasions as a synonym for something highly unpleasant. "Up the Down Staircase" I expected to be, if not neutral, at least on the right side: instead it proves to be extremely frivolous and at times downright racist. The other three books, *The Pearl*, *Ethan Frome*, and *The Old Man and the Sea* (especially the first and the last of these, since they are contemporary) seem to have that same criminal indifference [to the problems of race] that the newspaper articles had about Vietnam.

The fall semester 1968 in a rural Vermont high school brought home to me why racial and ethnic diversity is so vitally important—especially in education, because living in an ethnically and racially homogeneous society allows one simply to evade confronting the social and political questions that properly constitute part of any educational curriculum aspiring to prepare students for life in the world. George was recalled to California by his father along with the rest of the family before the start of the second semester. On January 24, 1969, I recorded in my journal:

> The realization that it is a relief to me that Gorge is leaving: I no longer need worry about making the course "relevant to the needs of the students." I can assign such irrelevant material as *Sweet Thursday*.

The "Irasburg Affair" was finally over, leaving me with what at one point the writer Norman Mailer called the most unpleasant feeling in life: not having risen to an occasion.

With Trina in Irasburg, Christmas 1968

2

BACK TO GRADUATE SCHOOL, 1969-1970

One of my colleagues at Lake Region Union High School was young Howard Frank Mosher, an aspiring writer in his mid-twenties and Superintendent Pelkey's fishing companion, who had been appointed to head the five-person English Department at the new school. Both he and his wife, Phillis, were among the most popular and successful teachers on the faculty. Howard was a no-nonsense kind of guy, very down-to-earth, and very sympathetic to student concerns. He commanded an enthusiastic following among the members of his college-bound senior English class. But Howard was determined to try his hand at writing as a career. For that purpose he decided to enroll in a creative writing course at one of the University of California campuses for the 1968-1969 school year. He recommended me as his successor to chair the department, bypassing Mrs. Elliott, who had headed the English Department at Orleans High School before the regional consolidation. I heard that Mrs. Elliott was quite disappointed, although she should have known from the fact that she was not selected the year before that in the new school youthful leadership would definitely be preferred.

As it turned out, Howard was quickly disenchanted with his creative writing course in California, and by the end of the year or shortly thereafter he was back in the "Northeast Kingdom", ready to make a go of it on his own. Howard, who had grown up in northern New York State, was genuinely fond of northern Vermont and its odd assortment of ornery French-Canadian and native Yankee character types, the protagonists of most of his books. He had a real talent for writing and a strong, firm bias in favor of unconventional, courageous, and principled behavior, the kind of traits he found to proliferate among the simple, unschooled, rural population of northern Vermont, their occasional craziness notwithstanding. Howard also had a strong rebellious streak that made him sympathetic to outcasts and outsiders of all kinds and served him well in his writing. His impatience with illegitimate authority would sometimes blend into intolerance for educated intellectual types, the only aspect of his writing that occasionally made me feel uncomfortable. But I remember how very impressed I was by the manuscript of short stories he gave me to read that was later published as *Where the Rivers Flow North*. In that manuscript I immediately recognized the born writer, committed to his craft by his innermost nature, it seemed. I was especially impressed by the fact that he had actually accomplished with discipline and will power what I had vainly set out to do at his age when I had returned to Europe in 1962.

Howard did have a strong romantic streak that sometimes led him to sentimentally idealize the denizens of his "Kingdom County," an amalgam of the three counties, Orleans, Essex, and Caledonia that make up what is still referred to as the "Northeast Kingdom" today. In 1989 he published a highly fictionalized account of the "Irasburg Affair," entitled *Stranger in the Kingdom*, which was eventually turned into a film as well. Out of an incident of run-of-the-mill rural racial prejudice Howard made a complex and exciting murder mystery in which, however, his heroes were just a bit too good and his villains just a bit too evil to ring true. Mama was affronted by his writing, insisting that he had got the distinctiveness of Vermont natives all wrong. "New Englanders are the most bigoted people in the world," she claimed. "They came as Puritans knowing they were better than anyone else, and they still do. It's their strength. It's what makes them so attractive. The typical Vermonter is shrewd, mean, and miserly—and makes a go of everything he touches." Even though Howard's romanticized version of the Irasburg Affair bore little resemblance to the mundane original, I was flattered when he told me that my thesis had given him some inspiration.

The notoriety accruing to the Northeast Kingdom as a result of the Irasburg Affair undoubtedly had its advantages as well. In December 1968 our principal Millard Harrison told me about one-year "Leadership Development Grants" offered by the Ford Foundation to potential leaders in rural backwaters with the goal of strengthening local leadership, promoting economic growth and educational reforms, and combating the effects of the continuing agrarian decline. At least the Irasburg Affair certified our status as "backward," as did the fact that the road leading to Lake Region Union High School was still unpaved at the time. I had the distinct impression that the fortuity of living in Irasburg played a key role in my selection as a Ford Fellow. The Ford Foundation of course hoped that the leaders it selected would return to their hometowns after their fellowship years to apply their newly-gained skills for the benefit of the community, but in my case the fellowship served as the catalyst for my return to graduate school and my liberation from the grind of teaching high school. Ironically, the unstructured nature of the fellowship program, in which grant recipients were encouraged to follow their interests and predilections, worked against the return of Ford fellows to the locales from which they had been selected. I recorded my reaction to the planning conference I attended in Farmington, Maine, in June, 1969:

I went to the conference feeling "up tight" (a phrase that seems distressingly coined to fit my particular condition) about what would be expected of me during my fellowship year. It was therefore exciting to hear both Ralph Bohrsons's remarks on leadership and Marv Rosenblum's on his experiences during his fellowship year. Bohrson spoke of persons capable of handling the changes that were occurring and would occur in the coming years. Rosenblum spoke of the change that he had gone through involving not his ideas or methods, but his whole personality. The greatest benefit of the Ford grant had been freedom, time, the opportunity to do just what he wanted to. He pleaded for as little "structuring" as possible. "That's how things happen." His most marvelous experience—the cultural shock of Hawaii—had been possible because his mentor had been unexpectedly delayed for six weeks and he (Marv) had been entirely on his own. He had been married at the outset of his fellowship year. "It was a one-year honeymoon. I recommend a Ford fellowship for all newly-weds." "People talk about imposing change on the system, but do not realize that the essential change must come within themselves... I'm coming to think that change for the sake of change is a good thing... Many changes can be made without money. And another thing. Let's not exaggerate the risk. Few of us run the risk of losing our jobs. We run the risk of being disliked. And this is a hard thing. One wants to be liked by everyone, and this just isn't possible." I would like to have known what he was like before his fellowship year. Could the grant have effected as much change as he gives it credit for?

The marvelous cynicism of Charlie Colcorde and the older grantees and their advice on expense account padding: "it's a one-year vacation. Enjoy it! . . . Face it. The Foundation's got to spend their money or they can't keep their tax-free status." Bohrson: "You are potential leaders, who have not yet been recognized as such, and in some cases may not even have recognized yourselves as such." Rosenblum: "The Ford fellowship allowed me to recognize the difference between my private person and my public image."

Rosenblum was an articulate advocate of the "sensitivity training" that was just coming into its own as part of the youthful counterculture of the late 1960s. "You're not doing anybody a favor by sparing them," Rosenblum insisted, "by not telling them your honest opinion. Advertising has made millions from the fact that nobody tells you you have bad breath and everyone assumes he has it." In retrospect, perhaps, the ubiquitous "encounter groups" that seemed to spring up everywhere were more a reaction to than an expression of the counterculture, but there is no denying the strong appeal that this rebellious and brutally honest new sensibility had for me. Under the dispensation of these new values, it seemed, it was OK to speak your mind and show your emotions. No longer were you compelled to do what was expected rather than what your conscience or your instinct or your inclination told you to do. Conventional norms were no longer binding in the new, more natural, more humane society the youthful rebels were trying to create. Now it was OK to let it all hang out and to do your own thing. Although at 34 I was almost twice as old as the "Woodstock generation," I heartily identified with their outlook. In many ways, it seemed to me, the student movement, the hippies, and the "sixties generation" had succeeded in breaking out of the stifling conformism that my own "fifties" generation had been fighting to overcome for too many years.

The mentor I was assigned to for my Ford fellowship year was Arleigh "Dick" Richardson, the director of a small government-sponsored agency called the National Humanities Faculty whose famous cousin, Elliott Richardson, would later resign his position as attorney general in Richard Nixon's cabinet rather than follow his boss's instruction to fire the special prosecutor in the Watergate Scandal, Archibald Cox. The National Humanities Program recruited university professors to visit secondary schools to give lectures to teachers and students. Dick Richardson invited me to accompany him on a ten-day trip in April to San Antonio, San Francisco, and Seattle to visit various schools and monitor their progress in establishing new humanities courses. In San Francisco I had the chance to visit my cousin Ellen Fleenor (born Edmonds) whose husband was completing on-the-job training at one of the San Francisco department stores in preparation for his return to his hometown in Boise, Idaho, to run the large family retail business. Interdisciplinary humanities courses were all the fashion in 1969. My Ford fellowship was to be devoted to learning about these new kinds of courses, which seemed to promise a whole new direction in secondary education. Students would be humanized by their exposure to the arts, and their alienation from society—a growing problem in 1969—would be overcome. Interdisciplinary humanities seemed almost like a pedagogical silver bullet at the time.

Most of my fellowship year was to be devoted to learning about innovative humanities programs that had been or were being developed at various sites all across the land. This involved quite a bit of travel, but of the fun kind with all expenses paid. My main base of operation was Boston, from where I could commute to the historic town of Concord, where the National Humanities Faculty had its small four-person administrative office. I took the opportunity, of course, to visit Ralph Waldo Emerson's home, where I marveled at the sturdy rustic charm of his study with its huge oak desk at which he wrote his famous sermons. In the spring of 1970 Steffi and Trina joined me in Boston at a dingy one-bedroom student apartment at 230 Commonwealth Avenue with the shared toilet out in the hall. By that time we had started rather earnestly trying to have another child, having "wasted" more than two years in doing our best to prevent a pregnancy. Among our visitors on Commonwealth Avenue were Fritzi and her daughter Andrea, recently returned from Europe. Not having any living room furniture (or even a living room), we had to sit on the edge of the bed. "Isn't it funny?" Fritzi said, with a glance at the dingy furnishings. "You were always the bright one and were supposed to be the big success in the family. But it is Olaf who turned out to be the successful one." Tact was never Fritzi's strongest suit.

Meanwhile, Betsy had fallen in love with Alvin Shulman, a violinist and instructor at Lyndon Institute, the local state college in neighboring Lyndonville, twenty miles southeast of Irasburg. Alvin was the older brother of my young colleague Marty Shulman, who taught at Lake Region as well. In June 1969 Betsy and Alvin got married in a civil ceremony at Marty and his wife Carol's home in Barton. Marty announced a "welcome to Shulmanland" and assured me that his family had no objections to his brother's marriage to a non-Jewish wife. Betsy converted to Judaism and became much more active in the small Lyndonville Jewish community than her more secularly-minded husband. Their common interest in music (Betsy taught music at several local primary and secondary schools) seemed to augur well for a happy marriage. Betsy's older twins, Chris and Julie, on the other hand, faced a bit of an adjustment. They complained to their mother that they could never tell whether Alvin was joking or not. "Just ask him," she advised; "he'll tell you." Alvin did begin to lay down the law, which even at times rubbed us adults the wrong way. We were no longer to discuss the Vietnam War in front of the children, because they were supposedly too young to understand. And, much to Steffi's dismay, German was no longer to be spoken at family gatherings.

Another major event that June was the ordination of our cousin Johnny Edmonds into the Episcopalian priesthood in South Weymouth, Massachusetts, not far from his mother's home in Andover. We used the occasion, too, to visit his older brother Nick at his backyard studio and received a guided tour of his latest massive creations, carved out of huge tree trunks that had been delivered directly from the lumber mill to his studio. Aunt Temple had sold the family farm on Reservation Road after Uncle John's death in 1965, and she now lived in an isolated house in a forested area on the banks of a local reservoir. Active and enterprising as always, she worked the night shift at the Boston City Hospital. One day, however, she returned home dead tired in the morning only to find that her alpha dog had killed one of the subordinate dogs in her pack. One source of the conflict between the dogs was their rivalry for Aunt Temple's affections, leading me to record the following reflection in my journal: "Mama's animals die of want or neglect; Aunt Temple's of competition and jealousy."

In July 1969 Steffi's father, his second wife Elisabeth, and his 9-year old son Johannes visited us in Vermont.

With Elisabeth, Johannes, and Trina, summer 1969

Gerhard Heuss had a gratifyingly high opinion of me. *"Du bist ein Tiefstapler,"* he told me, using a term (*Tiefstapler*) for which there is no precise equivalent in English to describe someone who understates his qualifications (as opposed to *Hochstapler* or "con man"). But he also gave his daughter due credit for the improvement in our fortunes: *"Das hättest du dir doch nicht träumen lassen,"* he said to me, *"in deiner Bruchbude in Berlin, dass du in zwei Jahren so ein schönes Heim haben würdest, was?* (in your wildest dreams you wouldn't have imagined, in your dump in Berlin, that in two years you'd have such a beautiful home, would you)? Yes, what all one can't accomplish with such a wife! The energy she generates, it shames one, and inspires one to action." Both Steffi and I were impatient, however, with the laxness with which he and Elisabeth were bringing up their son: "The boy is unbearably fresh to both his parents," I wrote in my journal. "It makes one want to give all three of them a good slap in the face."

In August all of us crammed into our tiny car, an early-model Corvair, famously condemned by Ralph Nader for its lack of safety, for a three-day trip to picturesque Quebec City. Its commercialization, however, struck us the wrong way.

Steffi on the demeaning treatment accorded to tourists: nowhere treated as persons, everywhere exploited and despised. The boy who came rushing up to wash our windshield while we parked for one minute to watch the falls at Montmorency. The girl who sold us the watercolor postcards probably thought of us, Steffi said, only as potential buyers. On all sides surrounded by tourist traps—restaurants, souvenir shops, horse-drawn carriages, "museums," etc. A kind of second-class citizenship. [Tourists] cannot presume to be taken seriously or treated as persons.

I combined our visit to Quebec with an interview with a M. Mackey of the Bilingual Center at Laval University, as bilingual education, along with the humanities curriculum, was to be the other major focus of my fellowship year. However, M. Mackey did not talk about bilingual research, as I had expected, but about French Canada in general.

It is the language, and only the language, that will preserve their cultural identity. French Canada is dynamic and growing. Unable to expand east or west, it has traditionally expanded north and south. The French in New England will preserve their language and culture only if there is communication with Canada. Small minorities have successfully maintained their language only where they have been able to lean on a strong neighbor—as for instance in the case of Switzerland.

On our way home Steffi's father delivered his verdict on our idyllic Vermont way of life: "*Maisfelder bearbeiten, alles schön und gut, aber es fehlen die nötigen Spannungen* (cultivating the cornfields, all very well, but the necessary tensions are missing)." He compared his visit to Vermont to turning the pages in a picture book, a pleasure evidently magnified by the fact that he wasn't forced to live here all the time.

Steffi and I, on the other hand, were entirely happy in the lush verdancy of Vermont, however remote it might be from the excitement of more urban areas. I spent many happy hours putting in a huge vegetable garden by hand on the site where the barn and its outbuildings had collapsed several years before. The large garden plot proved astonishingly fertile, a function no doubt of the plentiful rotting organic matter, which included substantial amounts of well-rotted cattle manure from the former stable. Despite a two-week dry spell in August our harvest exceeded all expectations. That year I also put in a few strawberry plants which spread rapidly and bore full fruit in the three or four summers that followed. In 1970 and 1971 we had enough strawberries to supply family, neighbors, and Ray's general store, which sold them to the public for a small commission.

Steffi and Trina on the back porch, summer 1970

Steffi's mother Lilo and her second husband, Hans Thümmler (1906-2002), came to visit in September 1969, bringing with them at our request a Volkswagen bug that would have cost us much more if we had had to buy it over here. Lilo and Hans were going to use it to take a little driving tour around New England and then leave it for us when they returned to Germany later in the fall. Tümmi, as Steffi called her step-father, had a badly compromised history as an enthusiastic member of the Nazi Party and the SS. Trained as a lawyer, he had served as a judge in military courts-martial, condemning a number of ordinary Wehrmacht soldiers to death for defeatism in the closing stages of the war. For this he was interned after the war, but was released in 1948, and in the Allied-sponsored amnesties of the early 1950s the charges against him were dropped. Tümmi returned to civilian life as an executive at the renowned Zeiss Optical company, now headquartered in Aalen in the state of Baden-Württemberg where he met and married Steffi's mother. She rather apologetically explained her decision to remarry as motivated by the desire not to become a burden to her daughters in her old age. But Tümmi was never able in his long life to entirely escape his past. Because the statute of limitations on serious war crimes was abolished in Germany in 1979, his case was periodically reopened. As late as the 1990s the attorney-general of the state of Baden-Württemberg had plans to resume Thümmler's prosecution.

Our lush garden.

When I first met Hans Thümmler in 1966 he had become a conservative pillar of post-war German society. Prosperous, graying, and heavy-set, he exuded an aura of confidence and bourgeois solidity. His views seemed narrow-minded and old-fashioned, to be sure, but otherwise entirely conventional. I did not feel comfortable with him, but not so much because of his Nazi past, which seemed almost unreal to me, but because his present-day politics were so different from mine. A staunchly anti-communist member of the

Christian Democratic Union (CDU), he was predictably critical of the protest movements of the 1960s, but not without a certain satisfaction that the United States was now also incriminating itself (in Vietnam) as his own country had done on a so much greater scale during the Second World War. Tümmi had a somewhat unexpected aesthetic streak, delighting in beautiful objects, admiring well-designed buildings, and eager to visit museums. *"Ich bin ein Büchernarr"* (I am a book-fiend), he told me. "I love books with beautiful bindings." He seemed to be an exemplar of Walter Benjamin's famous reference to fascism as the "aestheticizing of politics". On October 4th I recorded the following impression in my journal:

Trina picking strawberries, June 1971

Amazing! Tümmi, the ex-Nazi, SS man, *"kein Freund der SPD* (no friend of the Social Democrats)," loves Henry Miller! But why not? He loves the folksiness, the animalistic (in a positive sense) masks-off aspect, the sexual sordidness (*"jeder hat so seine eigenen Erfahrungen gemacht* [everyone has had his own experiences]")—perhaps it gives meaning to his own sordid experiences—the absence of introspection (but plenitude of "philosophizing"), the nihilistic hedonism: nothing is bad, if it is enjoyable: the emptiness of traditional values (and haven't they let Tümmi down, though he can never really lose them!). And he loves what we all love—Henry Miller's lack of embarrassment, perhaps even his mischievous delight in shocking the fearful and the virtuous. And Tümmi has something of that quality I have always sensed in Henry Miller: a basic distrust that people might look down on them, a distrust of all "superiority". Is it this "healthy", self-strengthening resentment, hatred, bitterness, that appeals most to Tümmi?

Olaf on a visit, summer 1970

That autumn I visited Wini in her tiny apartment on top of the flower store in Salisbury for the first time since I had left for Germany ten years before. She and her son Johnnie had already visited us in Vermont the previous year. Of course we talked about Mama and reminisced about the past. We speculated on what effect the war might have had on Mama. That it had had an enormous effect seemed indisputable. "The war threw me into dungarees," Mama said of herself. And in fact I can't remember Mama ever wearing a skirt or a dress except on very rare occasions, such as the Emmet wedding we attended in New York in the late 1940s or early 1950s. Wini wondered whether Mama's domestic and sartorial negligence, which had become ever more pronounced over the years, might not have been due to the fact that she had done too much during the war.

> "She kept us all going. She had none of that fear, that panic, that everybody had. And she shared everything. This was very unusual, you know. Most people kept everything for themselves, and they couldn't understand that with four children Mama wasn't worried about food. At that time the house wasn't dirty. Only once I remember being surprised when she opened a bureau drawer that it was so messy. But she had no animals at that time, and animals are dirty."

We talked about Wini's trip to Zurich in 1944, and her decision to return to Ried, despite the residency permit procured for her by Ying, the Chinese attaché to Switzerland and an old friend from Berlin days.

> "I couldn't just sit there [in Switzerland] doing nothing. So I went back. They thought I was crazy. Then Sweetie invited us to the Elmhof, and I persuaded Mama to go. If I hadn't talked her into it, Mama probably wouldn't have gone. Maybe it was a mistake, I don't know. It was terrible for Claire [Massenbach]. [Her son] Peter saw us leaving with our *Leiterwagen* (we had to walk to Bichl, you know) and he said he felt awfully lonely."—"Why did you want to leave Ried?" I asked.—"I was disliked. Brummer [the local grocer] hated me. I was too openly anti-Nazi. I couldn't understand the Bavarian dialect. Your mother was well-liked. She understood those people and got along with them well."

Wini, who had taken up painting seriously a few years before, had just opened an exhibition at a gallery in New York. I couldn't help but laugh at the distortion of history contained in the announcement of the exhibition put out by the gallery in an effort to stimulate public interest: "She chose as her place to work quiet Salisbury, Connecticut, where one has time! Desiring complete artistic independence she opened a small flower shop on Main Street." I knew, of course, that she would always be in Mama's debt, a realization that conferred a certain psychological strength. It was in fact Mama who had originally bought the flower shop and given it to Wini when she gave birth to her son John in October 1951. Wini claimed to want to get out of "the flower work" entirely, but said that she couldn't find anybody to run the business. She did not want to turn over running the shop to her employee, dependable though she might be. "Suzy is very good, but she is too ignorant to be a manager. She doesn't have enough education for that." Her son Johnnie had grown into a very attractive eighteen-year-old, now a student finishing his senior year at Salisbury School. "He's a little bit of a snob," Wini told me. "He doesn't like to work. 'You don't understand the young generation, Mommy,' he says to me. 'We're different from your generation.' Of course," Wini concluded, pensively; "everybody is a snob in some way."

On New Year's Eve 1969 poverty and negligence produced another potentially tragic mishap in Mama's life. Her self-constructed jerrybuilt shack, where Steffi and I had spent our amorous summer of 1967, burned to the ground. Mama had moved back to her shack several months before when relations with Connie became excessively antagonistic. Mama was barely able to escape the fire in her underclothes by cutting through the plastic sheathing she had used to construct a make-shift lean-to greenhouse on one side of the shack. She had difficulty piercing the heavy plastic and thought she was going to die. "So this is the way," she thought. "It was as if a voice were saying, 'Come this way, route 60, not route 70'." She scrambled up the hill to her neighbors half a mile away, who drove her to our house at about ten at night. I felt partly responsible for the disaster, because we had not invited Mama to spend this holiday evening with us, even though we lived only six miles away. Steffi had begun to resent what she took to be Mama's excessive influence on me. Instead we had invited young guests from the National Humanities Faculty office in Concord who had come to ski at Jay Peak. Among the victims of the fire was our dog "Puppsy," whom we had entrusted to Mama for temporary safekeeping. She had tied her next to the stove where the dog had no chance to escape. Mama's several farm animals—pigs, goats, and a cow—survived in a separate barn distant enough not to have caught fire (unlike her 1963 fire, when the barn was attached to the house). Mama did lose all of her sparse furnishings and all of her many books, as well as enough animal feed to have lasted until spring. I also blamed myself for not having prevented the fire. It was not as if I hadn't foreseen the danger. Water dripped from the ceiling on to the Christmas tree lights, and her logs were stacked high all around the stove, ostensibly to dry, but they were dry enough to catch fire. However, I decided that even a fire might be preferable to the consequences that might result if I persisted in my tiresome warnings. I felt it was a risk she was quite aware of, especially in view of her previous experience with fire, which had also occurred on one of the coldest nights of the year. Obviously she was quite prepared take the risk, perhaps reassured by the thought that lightning doesn't strike in the same place twice. Even if she seemed to be inviting an accident, I didn't feel it was my place to intervene. Our relationship was not one in which I could give her advice on how to run her mini-farm.

Trina on Mama's farm, 1970

While alone in Boston, before Steffi and Trini joined me after Christmas, I could not resist the temptation of revisiting Blackwood Street and Crusher

Casey's, the bar where I had spent so many hours drinking with Terry Fortes and her friends. I was unable to track her down, however; people at Casey's had heard of her but could not give me any information as to her present whereabouts. Demographically the area had changed. What had been a mixed residential area was now almost exclusively African-American. Children were playing in the street just as on the day when we arrived from Cambridge with Nick's station wagon. But there were no white children now.

With Trina in Boston, winter 1969-1970

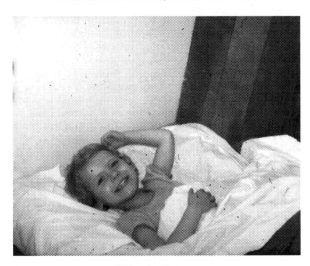

Trina in Boston

Living in Boston finally gave me a chance to reestablish contact with my Harvard roommate Paul Russell, now a successful psychiatrist affiliated with Beth Israel Hospital and enjoying an expanding private practice as well. His marriage to a fellow-physician with whom he had gone to medical school had broken up in some bitterness, apparently because his wife, under the influence of the burgeoning feminist movement, had become conscious of how unequal their relationship was. "She got tired of picking up after me," Paul told me. "I had always left my pajamas lying around, but suddenly this became grounds for divorce." His wife had gone to school with the poet Sylvia Plath and figured as one of the ill-disguised major characters in her memoir, *The Bell Jar*. Later Paul's ex-wife filed suit to have some unflattering references to herself deleted from the TV movie made of the book.

I found Paul now living in a new luxury apartment building in midtown Boston to which one could only gain entrance by passing through a security check. To me it seemed odd that anyone would want to thus publically signal their separation from surrounding society, but to Paul it seemed quite natural in a crime-ridden urban environment. When I finally contacted him, Paul told me of a recent dream in which I had made so vivid an appearance that he looked through the telephone book on the off-chance that I might be here in Boston! I found Paul unchanged, and certainly unspoiled, by success. His psychiatric training, or the habits of his practice, had reinforced those distinctive traits that made him so well-suited to this profession. In my journal I described these traits as "a tactical kind of listening, or rather, listening as tactic, and a patient kind of explaining." His mind was sharper than ever, though in my view directed too much to the goal of therapeutic adjustment to conditions as they were rather than social and political change.

My own political radicalization had continued in reaction to the Nixon Administration's continued prosecution of the Vietnam War, incisively analyzed in a series of long articles by Noam Chomsky in the *New York Review of Books* in 1969 and 1970, before that estimable journal closed its pages to such radical critiques. One of Chomsky's sentences in particular struck a chord with me: "The world's most advanced society has found the answer to people's war: eliminate the people." In November 1969 I was one of the approximately 100,000 persons who assembled on Boston Common to mark the Vietnam Moratorium. Boston University professor Howard Zinn gave a fiery talk in which he not only called for an end to the war, but optimistically envisioned the approaching socialization of American institutions. The countercultural "movement" seemed to be gaining ever greater momentum, and I was happy to be a part of it, even if I had never smoked "pot" up to that point in my life.

The books that I read in those days reinforced the radicalization of my views. The example of my student George Small, David Johnson's son who had taken his grandmother's name, first got me reading Eldridge Cleaver's *Soul on Ice*. I was amazed to discover how good it was, discovering thereby also my skepticism that a person with Cleaver's background could have written anything so good. I defended the book against Marty Shulman, who doubted whether Cleaver was the sole author. In any case he was totally out of sympathy with its message. "I believe in compensatory politics," Marty said, "compensatory economics, not in violence and revolution." Another strong influence was Paul Goodman, especially his *Growing Up Absurd* (1960) and *The New Reformation* (1970), which I first read in article form in the *New York Times Magazine*. From Paul Goodman I got my all-time favorite quote, condensing into one pithy sentence a point of view to which I continue to subscribe: "The repressed and excluded are always right in their rebellion, because they stand for our future wholeness." From a student of Paul Goodman's I read what I still consider one of the best books ever written about primary education, George Denison's *The Lives of Children* (1969). The best book on secondary education, I thought, was *Coming of Age in America* (1965) by Edgar Z. Friedenberg, whom I had the good fortune to meet at some of the many educational conferences I attended during my fellowship year. I transcribed his definition of integrity from *The Vanishing Adolescent* (1959) in my journal:

> Integrity is the power to use your real feelings to guide your actions in a real world that is refractory and densely populated with other persons whose goals and feelings must be recognized and respected. It operates as a delicate balance between subjectivity and objectivity, passion and self-discipline.

I was also impressed by the following quote: "Any individual through whom subjective intensity may intrude upon the processes of bureaucratic equilibrium is extremely threatening to our society." I was dismayed, however,

by his pessimism when I heard him speak in Toronto shortly after the killings
at Kent State on May 4th, 1970:

> No hope that even a revolution would produce the changes that we
> desire: it is the minority groups that get shot and killed. About the
> Kent State student killings: you'd think the people of Ohio would be
> disappointed in their National Guard—that the body count was not
> higher. Referring, perhaps, to the construction workers' riot in New York
> City and the police's failure to arrest or stop them: One had expected
> the coming of fascism in America to be more different from the models
> of the past.

My admiration for Friedenberg was undiminished, however, as attested by
the following entry in my journal in April 1970:

> He has, by dint of constant work, constant reiteration and reexamination
> of his beliefs, become a man who can stand up for them at any time.
> My article has shown me that I can gain this moral stature only during
> moments of insight, only at odd times—that my life has been (though
> it need not continue to be) corrupted by laziness, forgetfulness,
> compromise, repeated failure to act on my instincts or beliefs, repeated
> failure of integrity.

The article referred to in that entry was to become my first academic
publication, entitled "The Moral Purpose of Humanities Programs,"
published in the November 1970 issue of the *English Journal*. Presented as the
summation of my fellowship experience, the article was meant to be a protest
against the unending war in Vietnam and what I saw as the collaboration,
whether intended or not, of the educational establishment in the continuation
of that war. Dissenting from the self-congratulatory exaggerations of the
benefits to be derived from interdisciplinary humanities programs that
were the theme of so many conference presentations, I wanted humanities
programs to become a genuine vehicle of social critique and reform, not just an
exercise in socializing students and citizens into the existing social structure
by making students feel good about themselves. "It sounds like you want a
humanities program to be a journey into the heart of darkness," my brother-

in-law Alvin Shulman commented after reading the article. It seemed to me that the innovations advocated at these conferences had mainly the function of increasing the technical efficiency of humanistic education, not developing the ethical conscience that should be the foundation of such an education. "What is it the humanities movement is purveying?" I wrote in my journal. "Ostentatious enthusiasm for edifying slogans—the same old malady of society as a whole."

> Is the objective of education really only that Johnny (and Mary) be able to read better? Have we done our duty by Johnny if we have raised his reading ability to a point where he can pass the qualifying exams for the armed services and be sent to Vietnam to kill and be killed? Is it only ever greater educational efficiency we are after? That is the Eichmann syndrome, just do your duty without questioning the results. That is the attitude expressed by "what's wrong with security?" [a question posed by someone who objected to my criticism at one of the conferences I attended], an attitude responsible for most of our crimes. I see the planet teeming with little nests of security, with each person worrying about his own little nest, and making it bigger and better, usually at the expense of his neighbor, while the planet itself goes to hell.

This importunate thought formed the major theme of my article:

> A case in point is the treatment of war, an almost mandatory unit for humanities courses nowadays that want to be up-to-date. War is the most easily visible evil, and opposition to it is not likely to provoke disagreement in any quarter. Even the politicians and generals who make war are opposed to it (if only because they would much prefer to realize their aggressive designs without recourse to war). We take a stand, then, against war and say that the impulse toward war is an evil trait in man that we must seek to overcome or get rid of. We tend to blame wars and atrocities on the Hitlers, large and small, of the world (usually our enemies), and disregard the much more numerous Eichmanns, although (or perhaps because) there is a lot more of Eichmann than of Hitler in most of us. We do not analyze how wars result from our own normal everyday virtues, our aggregate efficiencies,

our dutifully executed routines, our functions which we dignify with the word "responsibilities," our modesty (the positive form of timidity), our goodwill, our cooperativeness, our sense of order and propriety, our decency, our respectability, yes, our humanity. By implication we do not admit that we are responsible at all. War is some lurking evil in mankind. We fight it in the moral sphere, by pledging our abhorrence. When asked to eradicate it in fact, we reply that that is, after all, not the job of the schools.

Technology is another fashionable bugaboo. It is not hard to see that we will never achieve the objectives we claim to espouse if we seek the source of our troubles outside ourselves. It is not technology, but the technocratic frame of mind—a frame of mind admittedly fostered by technology, but by no means restricted to it—that produces and permits the social maladies that we are all united, at least in words, in opposing. There are technocrats in every walk of modern life, and most emphatically in the humanities, too: people who see their jobs, whatever they be, not in their larger moral context, but as functions to be carried out with ever greater efficiency. It is ridiculous, of course, to suppose that a person should be more "humane" (less susceptible to such vices as bureaucratism, careerism, professional vanity, and the intellectual vices of jargon, intellection, and abstraction) just because one is active in the field of humanities. But the rhetoric of the humanities does throw a certain hypocritical aspect into relief...

Perhaps the problem boils down to a basic lack of commitment. Perhaps it is not just coincidental that most humanities programs speak of man in the third person, of "*his* achievements and problems, *his* past and present," as if they were speaking of a species to which the administrators of the program did not belong. What commitment there is, is to the program, not to man. Small wonder, then, that the program develops a life of its own, develops the same showcase quality, the same formal objectivity, the same exaggerated sense of its own importance, as all the other programs that have preceded it. The program itself becomes one of man's problems—and an obstacle to the humanistic values it literally feeds on. The humanities become just another vehicle to the kind of success to which we owe our deepest commitment, and the humane values, to which we pay such fancy lip service, turn out to be simply the morality most compatible with this success.

Whatever we may say in our course guidelines, we do not, by and large, examine our moral values; we profess them. Our humanities courses, by and large, are in search and pursuit of goodness, not awareness. They are designed to do for the spirit what physical education does for the body: strengthen it. They do so with pretty much the same type of determination and fall into most of the same traps (accent on winning, exhibitionism, pep rallies, downgrading of individual idiosyncrasy in favor of the team). Most ominous of all is perhaps the competition in enthusiasm that facilitates placing the blame for eventual miscarriages on those who show less. It is the same kind of subtle, and not so subtle, pressure that established institutions exert against dissent. Woe unto him who does not at least claim to love people, though he may only love his success with people, or hate being alone, or wish to ingratiate himself.

To complement the brash self-confidence of the football field, humanities guidelines propose to develop what is called "self-concept." It is a much safer and more positive term than the one in the dictionary—self-consciousness. Self-concept suggests that a person think favorably of himself, self-consciousness that he understand himself. But self-consciousness suggests also the insecurity that a person must feel when one becomes conscious of one's motives, intentions, desires. (A linguistic analysis of why self-consciousness has received such a negative connotation in English might shed some light on our cultural values. My own theory is that it has gotten this connotation because it impedes activity—and activity is a prerequisite to success. Self-consciousness slows decision—though not necessarily ethical decisions, which without self-consciousness, are generally never made at all.) There isn't a person in the country, including the most narrow-minded and bigoted, who hasn't learned to dress his prejudices in the most winning garments. The humanities ought not to make it easier for us. It ought not hand us the garments; it ought to rip them off us.

What are the practical consequences of what I have said?... The humanities must become more radical, more socially, politically, economically, psychologically aware. It does not mean that we must go out in the streets and demonstrate. It simply means that we get off our high moral horse and back on to the plane of reality, that we once again substitute analysis for enthusiasm, and criticism for reverence and piety. It means that we encourage, both for students and teachers, an examination of our present life, of our present activities—and not just to find more streamlined methods of operation. Let us not give up our moral purpose, let us fulfill it, not by celebrating the values we call humane that lead to success, but by analyzing the ultimately pernicious consequences of some of these very values. The moral life is not just "being good" or "loving man"; it is continuous hard work. The extremely human traits of laziness, forgetfulness, complacency, opportunism, self-deception thwart it at every turn.

Let us enter into areas that are presently taboo... Let us ask embarrassing questions. Let us ask why nations, and those responsible for national policy, do not respect the values we have found to work in personal relations. Why is it quite acceptable for nations to be arrogant, self-seeking, and boastful? Why is a politician sure to find approval if he justifies his acts as in the self-interest of the nation, no matter how immoral these might otherwise be? And let us call a spade a spade. The name of the human game as we presently play it and as we seem constituted to play it is power—power in all its variations. The humanities in the schools—if they are serious about correcting the abuses of power—should not allow themselves to become simply the arsenals of moral weaponry that help us to pursue this game with greatest success.

Our young people are trying to tell us this. I deliberately use the word *trying*, because I am convinced there are literally millions of young people in this country who feel this sense of discomfort and alienation, who feel in their bones that they are surrounded by sham, delusion, and hypocrisy, even while we tell them to be honest, respectful, and decent. But it is only the fortunate few who can put their fingers on the trouble, who can tell what is bothering them, who really are aware of what is bothering them. Is it not our task, the task of the humanities, to help them get to the source of this alienation, not to dismiss it with lofty sentiments about man, but to pinpoint and act upon it? Not to add to the smoke screen of comfortable delusions, but to dispel it? Not to make us feel good about ourselves, but to make us aware of ourselves?

Forty years later the sexist language that seemed quite normal in that still male-dominated age is certainly embarrassing, but the article's activist political philosophy reflected the temper of the times and continues to accord with my left-oriented political attitude today. I found plenty of corroboration for my views in the alternative press that proliferated in those years. In April 1970 I quoted one such passage:

Picking up the *Village Voice,* feeling guilty for killing time, finding the following excerpt that fits right in with the article I am writing: [it spoke of] "the smokescreen of delusions that allow too many Americans to cling to the pious belief that if only we could treat each other with honesty and respect and the decency that dwells within us, everything would be all right. And until that smokescreen is dissipated, too many Americans will continue to wait for the full flowering of our latent humanity rather than work up the political will to confront the results of our inhumanity."

But I also came to realize that it is much easier to preach activism than to practice it:

Another thing my article shows me (is there anything that doesn't show me?) is that I am again and again criticizing something in myself, or to put it another way, I am again and again guilty of the very things I am criticizing.

Not political activism, but de-politicization—citizen apathy—seemed to me to be the true source of the problems we faced as a society. Maintaining the activism and idealism of the civil rights and anti-war movements would prove to be the major challenge of the 1970s, one that became particularly daunting after President Nixon ended the draft and created the all-volunteer professional army in 1973. Young people seemed to lose interest in trying to end the war. The "movement" fragmented and gradually dissolved in the course of the 1970s, leaving the field clear for the resurgence of a conservative backlash that culminated in the election of Ronald Reagan in 1980.

In the spring of my fellowship year I made the decision to return to graduate school, with Steffi's encouragement, but not without a strong feeling of guilt for thus abandoning the teaching post at Lake Region that had made me eligible for the fellowship in the first place. Dick Richardson had been right when he pinpointed the main problem facing the administrators of the Ford Foundation fellowships: "How do you keep them down on the ranch once they have seen the world?" While most of the fellowship recipients did return to their former careers, prepared to put their newly-acquired training at the service of their communities, I used the opportunity to try to move on to teaching on the college level. My real motive was to try to pursue my frustrated writing ambitions, which I knew I would never do unless forced to do so by professional obligations. My years of teaching experience helped me to get a graduate assistantship at the University of Vermont in Burlington, on the west side of the state. This not only made graduate school affordable, but also had the advantage of keeping us close to our beloved home in Irasburg.

Our driveway in Irasburg

Steffi would open a shop in the living room of our home in 1971 for which I provided the wood paneling and the shelves. Her exquisitely designed jewelry was attracting growing numbers of customers, assuring us of an additional income.

Steffi's shop in Irasburg

And so, fourteen years after abandoning Columbia, and ten years after forsaking Harvard, I resumed my graduate training—this time in history, a field that I expected to give me greater incentive to write for publication than language or literature.

3

BURLINGTON, VERMONT, 1970-1971

Steffi and Trina spent the academic year 1970-1971 with me in Burlington at an apartment at 43 South Winooski Avenue, within walking distance of the UVM campus. Our landlady, a dour-looking woman in her fifties, was quite suspicious of us when we first looked at the apartment in early August. She apparently had had some bad experience renting to students in the past. The beard that I had started to grow by that time may have added to her suspicions. She was somewhat reassured by the fact that Steffi was German. "Cleanliness is a German national trait, isn't it?" she asked. Four-year old Trina helped overcome the landlady's qualms by ingenuously asking her, "Which bed is mine?" Trini also was the only one of us three who would not have minded staying in Burlington right then and there. For Steffi and me renting an apartment was a painful exercise, reminding us that we were also giving up, at least temporarily, a way of life centered on our home in Irasburg. To me it also seemed final proof that I would never fulfill my creative writing ambitions.

Later that year, in November, our house became the source of a terrible row with David and Jean LaRoche, back from a year's tour of duty with an American aid agency in Laos, which turned out to be a front for the American government's expansionist policies in Asia. David was very active that summer in the failed Senate election campaign of former governor Phil Hoff, for whom we had given, at David's request, a well-attended house party in Irasburg. After the unexpected disappointment of Hoff's defeat in November, David and Jean asked if they could stay in our house in Irasburg for about two weeks until they had figured out their future plans (which eventually took

David to a well-paying legislative staff position in Washington DC). Steffi was very unhappy at the prospect of their staying in her home while we were in Burlington. To her the idea of somebody else living there seemed, if not a defilement, at the very least a violation of our privacy. Although at heart I agreed with her, it was impossible to say no. Denying good friends such a modest request would have given the lie to our protestations of solidarity and friendship, especially as they also offered to pay rent. But Steffi adamantly refused to accept any money for fear of legitimizing and perhaps prolonging their stay. In my journal I analyzed my disagreement with Steffi:

In Burlington, 1970-1971

The ease with which I was *überrumpelt* (taken unawares) made things worse. It appeared [to Steffi] that I wanted only to play the role of magnanimous benefactor. And it is true that I could have refused David's request only on the grounds of a selfish property fetishism that David probably knew I could not afford to embrace.

It was useless to try to persuade Steffi that a house serves just a utilitarian function, that it did no damage to have people living in it, that in fact it was good for the house. Her attitude toward the house, to objects in general, is much too aesthetic for that. Each object, even as mechanical an object as the stove, has its own intrinsic aesthetic value: it is there not only to be used, but also to be appreciated. If it is used in a purely utilitarian spirit it is devalued and profaned. Though she is worried about possible dirt (especially from their dog and cat), it is the spiritual devaluation that seems to weigh most heavily. In her mind everything is fragile, delicate, though when pressed to give an example, she cannot think of one. A radical refurbishing is now her only hope. "*Ich werde alles rausreissen und neu streichen* (I'm going to tear everything out and paint it new)," she said. "And then I'm going to stay there and then I never want to see you again." By my action I had denied the sanctity and integrity of "home."

Trina at the piano in Irasburg, 1970

What hurts, too, is the realization that what we would like to do but can't—live at home in Irasburg—others can. It throws into bitter relief the dissatisfaction of our present way of life. It questions the very premise of a happy life—that one is doing what one wants to—while showing us how apparently easy it is to do what one wants to do.

And so, with all-too-evident reluctance, we gave the LaRoches permission to move in. But things did not go well.

David's distressingly "political" side: calling to say that they had finished moving in and that everything was OK: I asked him if the broiler was on, and he said, yes, supper was cooking and all was fine. A moment later, after Jean had said something, he was forced to retract: "Could you repeat your instructions on the gas? There's no gas coming in." Apparently he had simply left the lighting of the stove to Jean, who must have said she knew how. His primary interest was to reassure me. Political principle number one: give the people what they want; make them think they're getting what they want; tell them what they want to hear.

The dispute with the LaRoches reached a terrible climax after they had moved out, under not-so-subtle pressure from us, around Thanksgiving. I tried to maintain our friendship but had underestimated the degree to which they had found our conduct humiliating. Here is how I described the climactic end of our friendship in a journal entry on December 4th:

At Steffi's insistence, I called Dave at 10 o'clock at night at the Moshers'. He was breathing audibly hard when he came to the phone, and I was struggling with myself, too. At first, he was content to follow Jean's example, or a pre-agreed plan, and spoke in a deliberately brusque and distant way. I asked, "Is anything the matter?" in order to have it out, but I should have waited until I had better control of myself. David said, "I'd like an explanation for the way you've treated us, the terse, unfriendly note, and so on." Without reflecting, I blurted out what I had been thinking, vaguely feeling all the time that I must not back down, as I seem always to have done in relations with David. "Since we have so little money ourselves, I don't see why we should support you."—"Support us? You support us? You'll *never* support us!" I tried to

retract, but it was too late. "You son of a bitch, Rodi. You son of a bitch."
And he hung up. I tried to get him on the phone again, apologizing to
Jean and explaining that I had not meant it that way, and had obviously
chosen the wrong word in the heat of the discussion. But Jean only hung
up on me, too. "We've had enough of you. Goodbye, Rodi."

My dilemma was, though I wasn't aware of it at the time, that I could
not give the real reason for our unfriendliness, the reason Dave and
Jean were quick to sense: the fact that we (especially Steffi, of course)
didn't want anyone in our house. I had to find something wrong in
the LaRoches and clumsily fastened on what was bound to humiliate
him most. Now the whole hatred of his violent-prone temperament is
concentrated on me. His present employment predicament, robbing
him of his manhood, only aggravates his wound. Telepathy: sensing his
hatred, fearing his violence (the symbol of his shotgun shells lined up
on the bookshelf. In the old days, I suppose, I would, like Pushkin, have
died in a duel.) The sexual symbolism of his intrusion into the house;
also the symbol of bacteria and disease. My prophecy (in connection
with the unexpected rise of our property taxes), "There are bound to
be encroachments from outside."

How property breeds bourgeois values! How my radicalism cracks when
it is tested in actual practice! How our happiness and prosperity—our
house—seems to invite disaster!

And how those underneath, the repressed and excluded, are always
right!

Dave and Jean proceeding through life in a series of moral confrontations,
each one providing the energy for the next stage of life. Just after he
moved in to our house he proudly announced that he had turned down
an offer to teach English at North Country [in neighboring Newport]. It
does not seem to him, as it does to me, that it is proper to take any job
in order to pay your bills.

A few days later I added the following reflections:

What makes it so hard to bear is being in the wrong (particularly hard for someone who has tried to base his life on being in the right).

Realization that what makes David effective as an activist, as a political force, is that he won't allow himself to be pushed around in the world, whereas I accept that as an inevitable part of life.

And thus I managed by writing about it to somewhat alleviate the pain.

Before our move to Burlington, we had made another visit to Annie Fisher, who had just celebrated her 85th birthday. On August 12th I wrote the following commentary on our visit:

Again the surprise to find her so alert and healthy-minded (meaning ornery and independent). It explains how she can survive in that moribund atmosphere for so many years. "I am dying by inches." Lacking her mental stamina, the other old persons, whom Annie commandeers with absolute confidence, come in and get some strength from her. She has signed off her body long ago, seeming actually thereby to increase her ability to survive, since its vagaries have become somewhat irrelevant. Even though she was quite well able to get downstairs, she was very annoyed to have been pressured into it (for a birthday cookout on the front porch—her first time out in three years), and she obstinately refused to enjoy it. She still thrives on ther love-hate relationships with her various sets of former neighbors, notably the Bedards, who took down her fence and made a hotbed on her property. Thank God for us she defended it! She is marvelously free of self-pity, and even when she says, as she did twice, "Life is sad," she says it matter-of-factly and firmly, uncomplainingly. How different from old Mrs. Kahn, for whom I "baby-sat" in New York! She has certain stock jokes: "Body by Fisher," for instance, or "I had an operation on my jaw, but it didn't hurt my tongue any!" Her age puts things in perspective, too. She refers to Avis Harper, school board member and rather severe pillar of society, as "that little Harper girl." "She's an Irasburg girl, you know, Avis Pike. She's been very good to me." Even Doris Alexander [in her late sixties] is pushed down a generation.

That same August Olaf took me to visit a former colleague of his, the European historian Fred Krantz, now teaching at Concordia University in Montreal. Krantz had left Duke University out of protest against the Duke administration's hostility to the student movement. I recorded our visit in my journal on August 21st:

Impressions of visit to Fred Krantz in Montreal, former colleague of Olaf's at Duke where he was dismissed for his radical views: More Canadian than the Canadians. Struck by the suburban quality of his life, in such contrast to his alleged radicalism. "Showing off" not only the city of Montreal, but also the model apartments and shops in the rather exclusive complex where he lives (Ile de Soeurs). Apparently a rather doctrinaire Marxist: "Chomsky is the guru of the hippie youth today. He's too anarchist for me." Krantz is working on a modern European history text (to replace Palmer) from a Marxist point of view. "We have the most with-it department in America today... We've got quite an intellectual proletariat here." He was very depressing about Vietnam: "It looks like the U. S. is going to win. It looks like they're going to bring home the coon-skin. The revolution isn't going to take place. Vietnam will stay divided." He had an interesting theory about the First World War: "Germany should have won. Then there would have been a traditional settlement, like 1870." He had a deep-seated resentment against Duke and in fact the South. "I hate those southerners. I hate WASPS." Every time Olaf mentioned returning to Durham he laughed, reaching a peak in a kind of falsetto scream, reminiscent of Howard Mosher. Both he and Don Ginter, another "exiled" colleague, had a barely discernible contempt, not for Olaf, but probably for his lack of radicalism. Yet, though I agreed with everything they said, I was surprised how much I preferred Olaf as a person ...

Krantz and the French Canadians: He belittles the problem, or more exactly, seems unconcerned about it: "If the separatists win, it wouldn't affect us a bit. I might have to teach my courses in French, but that wouldn't matter." A quote from the *New York Review of Books* on the New School seems to apply to him: "Having fled persecution in their homelands, and having found a tolerable environment elsewhere, do they consequently evade all potentially embarrassing political involvement? Does their exile negate their engagement? The exile readily becomes an exilarch, that is to say, a sort of hereditary ruler in the place of exile, recapitulating the culture of the past so far as that is possible, while drawing strength from the mythos of persecution. At the same time the host society is held at bay...All is subordinated to the memory of the initial trauma."

As it turned out, Krantz would later follow a left-to-right ideological trajectory similar to David Horowitz's, though perhaps not quite so extreme. The erstwhile anti-war and civil rights activist became a staunch defender of the Israeli government, condemning critics of Israel's apartheid policies and denouncing as "terrorists" students demonstrating against an appearance of former and future Israeli Prime Minister Benjamin Netanyahu at Concordia University in September 2002. Promoted to the position of Director of the Canadian Institute for Jewish Research, Krantz, the former supporter of the 1960s student movement, came to see youthful rebellion in support of Palestinian rights as a dangerous harbinger of fascism. But there were already signs of his coming defection from progressive causes back when we visited him in August 1970:

Krantz voting for Nixon: at the time he told Olaf it was to undermine the system; now he defends it as saving North Carolina from Wallace.

He fears most of all that the student movement is open to demagoguery from the right. He is suspicious of the mass appeal of rock festivals.

His car—the one he sold to Olaf—says as much about him as his words: fitted out with frills and eye-pleasing extras as well as devices to enhance its power. "It's the biggest car on the road. I found out that for really very little extra money I could make it into something special."

And already then he subscribed to *The New Republic* "to keep up with the left libs."

As much as I enjoyed studying—what luxury to devote full time to intellectual activity and cultivating the mind—it was not at all easy at my age to return to the subordinate status of student. What made it even more difficult was that some of the profs who had joined the faculty in the rapid expansion of the 1960s were younger than I was. I did not know it at the time, but my later *Doktorvater* (dissertation supervisor) at the University of Massachusetts, the intellectual historian Will Johnston, had graduated from Harvard two years after I did! By the time I finished my dissertation in 1974 he had already published several books! On September 2nd I recorded my impressions of my first days back in a university setting:

Remanded by Professor [Wolfe] Schmokel for laughing when he said he didn't know anything about the course in German history he was going to teach: "That's an inside joke."

The disagreeable twosome of history profs at the sectioning meeting in the gym: the task—entering students into sections on a large chart—turned them into petty and pompous functionaries. And how docile the students were!

Peculiar kind of awe or fear that Schmokel and Overfield seemed to have of me: Schmokel recommended that I not take German history until the second semester, since he didn't feel he had enough to offer. Overfield discouraged me from attending his lecture, although presumably I will conduct a discussion group in his Western Civ course. Are they suspicious of me as a potential troublemaker?

The peculiarly strong difference that age makes in contact with students. I sometimes feel I belong to a different species.

Overfield, on taking the discussion sections himself, rather than having me lead them."They pay so much tuition, I want to give them their money's worth. I want to at least give them a professor." And this after I had said I understood perfectly wanting to conduct the discussion sections in one's own course. Overfield: "Oh no, it's nothing that selfish."

My feelings about returning to grad school at age 35 were ambivalent (an experience shared by so many women over the years who had devoted their twenties to raising a family). On the one hand I chafed under a hierarchical system that once again put me on the bottom rung at a time when my peers were becoming well established in their professional careers; on the other hand I understood that the perspective I gained "from below" and "from outside" gave me a certain psychological and perspectival advantage over those of my age cohort in academia who had never tasted failure and whose freedom of thought and political attitudes were constricted by institutional structures to which they had to submit if they wished to advance in the profession. Although I felt I was being held at arm's length by the faculty, this sense of exclusion was far outweighed by the delight I felt in finally having returned to a milieu that over the course of a lifetime would prove to be most congenial to my interests and aptitudes.

What do I remember from that year in Burlington? The local *cause célèbre* at UVM in the fall of 1970 was the student-led campaign in support of young Michael Parenti (b. 1933), a fierce critic of the Vietnam War, who had been denied tenure by the Political Science department. "Why aren't you indicted? Why aren't you in jail?" he challenged his faculty colleagues, many of whom also opposed the war, but the decision stood, and Parenti went on to a fine career as an investigative journalist and articulate critic of American imperialism.

My favorite class, or at least the most intriguing one, was an evening seminar given jointly by an Americanist, Jeremy Felt, and a Europeanist, Patrick Hutton. Felt, chairman of the department at the time, was a bit older than I was, and Hutton was a bit younger. I no longer remember the specific topic of the seminar, but in effect it was a comparative intellectual history course on certain ideas and ideologies in their American and European contexts. What made the course so interesting was less its content, though that was interesting enough, but rather the considerable variety and unconventionality of the students it attracted. One such character was a hippie girl named Gwen who always came to class with her well-behaved dog. One time she recommended LSD ("acid") for the straight-laced Mr. Hutton's cold! She was quite sincere: "It'll really get rid of it fast." Mr. Hutton was not one to take kindly to such scurrility, however. On December 11th I recorded his effort to put her in her place:

> Hutton at his meanest last Wednesday evening. The tall "hippy" girl
> Gwen teased him for being so traditional—the atmosphere in class was
> light and genial at the time. Hutton paused, and it was obvious that
> he was collecting himself for a riposte. "If you knew what the word

'traditional' meant," he said, with acid dripping from every word. Gwen did not speak again that class. The incident certainly proved that her criticism had found its mark.

I had my own troubles with Hutton the following spring when he downgraded a paper I had written on Rousseau for its inordinate advocacy of Rousseau's ideas of participatory democracy. One of the books Hutton had assigned in the course was *The Origins of Totalitarian Democracy* by J. L. Talmon, whose interpretation I criticized in my paper. Hutton had earned his PhD under George Mosse (1918-1999) at the University of Wisconsin and shared his mentor's political moderation and suspicion, at that stage of Mosse's career, of any challenges to middle-class values and conventions, whether from the left or the right. This fetishism of "balance" led me to the following rather sophistic reflection in my journal:

> The "golden mean" or "golden rule" does not reject "extremes," it validates them! It pays tribute to the fact that one's behavior is constantly modified by "extremes" and in the absence of this modification all behavior is extreme. You can define your view as "moderate" because there are "extremes."

Hutton had developed a specialization on the nineteenth-century French revolutionary leader Auguste Blanqui (1805-1881) on whom he later wrote a book critical of his ideas. Hutton and Felt evinced an easy and genial rapport in class, based in part on corporate solidarity.

> Felt and Hutton laughing gleefully at the thought that garbage collectors get paid more than college professors: "It looks like we chose the wrong profession."

Felt had rather different limitations than Hutton, which I analyzed as follows:

> The Felt syndrome: exposed for so long and on all sides to so much intellectual argumentation that his intellectual honesty no longer permits him to speak in anything but vague generalities and distinctions—such as optimistic vs. pessimistic. His confusion is genuine: because he sees so

much, he sees only a maze: hence, perhaps also, his suspicion of what he calls the New York Review of Each Other's Books, which he nevertheless conscientiously reads.

My most uncharitable summation of the Wednesday evening seminar I divulged only to my journal: "Mr. Glib (Hutton) and Mr. Simple (Felt) make up the team of Messrs. Superficial."

Despite Steffi's half-feigned objections to my studying German history—*"Du hast uns nicht zu studieren* (you have no business studying us)"—I had decided to make this my field of concentration, partly, of course, to achieve some clarity about my own background. The faculty member with whom I worked most closely was Wolfe Schmokel, the specialist for Germany in the UVM history department. He was a chain smoker, who unabashedly bummed cigarettes from his students right during class. Not surprisingly, he died of a heart attack while still in his fifties. Through his *Doktorvater* Hajo Holborn (1902-1969) at Yale via the celebrated historian Friedrich Meinecke (1862-1954) in Berlin, Schmokel proudly traced his disciplinary line of descent all the way back to one of the founders of historical scholarship, Leopold von Ranke (1795-1886), in the nineteenth century. A thoroughly self-made man, Schmokel had obtained American citizenship by joining the U.S. Army directly from Germany. He was recruited into a unit formed in response to the Cold War and made up of European displaced persons from the East. One year younger than Olaf, he graduated from college (the University of Maryland in Iceland!) one year after me. He had been at UVM since 1962 and had published a book on Nazi colonial ambitions in Africa in 1964. We differed on almost everything, from the Parenti case to the student movement, but got along very well nonetheless.

Schmokel on Parenti: "I have spoken to a student who told me, 'He preaches.'"

On the poster celebrating the Tet offensive, which Parenti had defended: "To glorify the victories of your enemy, that's going a little far."

"The trouble is that we take politics too seriously. We think that it can solve all questions. In politics there are no ends, only means."

He worried that the Parenti controversy would adversely affect town-gown relations in Burlington, which up to then had been very good. The conservative *Burlington Free Press* indeed missed no opportunity to cast aspersions on Parenti and the anti-war cause he represented. Schmokel was also highly critical of the student movement, going so far as to cite Heinrich von Treitschke at length in class on the unshaven, uncouth liberal youth of the 1820s and 1830s. Schmokel: "Some of the puny prophets of today might do well to look back at this period, the early nineteenth century, for a much better discussion of what is going on today." I saw his inclination to line up with power rather than to question it as the main difference between us. He, for his part, good-naturedly pronounced me to be "far gone."

What I liked about Schmokel, despite his limitations, was that he seemed to recognize something in me. It is this feeling that a teacher ought to convey to his or her student. Of course, it may only have been my aristocratic descent that he admired. That was certainly the case with his wife Varian, a socialite whose first husband was related to the Biddles. "We heard a lot about the von Stackelbergs," she said. Schmokel was impressed to have discovered, on his own, that one of our forebears had been the Russian representative to the Congress of Vienna in 1815. What Schmokel professed to hate most were intellectual snobs, whom he seemed to encounter with rather suspicious frequency. "I can remember my own revelation at Damascus very well," he told me.

> When I first got to Yale I was completely cowed. I had never been to college and I had always thought, if you have a historical problem, the way to solve it is to search for another fact, which is one perfectly valid approach to history. At Yale the other graduate students were talking about intellectual movements and concepts I had never even heard of. One day in a seminar the professor asked, "By the way, when was the Peace of Augsburg?" and nobody knew except little old me, and then I knew they were phonies.

Of course he hated the "New Left," which put him in a bit of a quandary in interpreting fascism. On the one hand he wanted to discredit the New Left by associating them with fascism; on the other hand, perhaps as a result of his family background, he sought to portray Germany's submission to fascism as not such an unnatural event. What seemed to anger him most was the Marxist concept of "false consciousness," which for him illustrated the presumption of intellectuals thinking they knew what was best for the working class. He defended the right of people to allow themselves to be deluded or seduced into supporting policies or embracing values that objectively were not in their own best interests. I thought a quote from C. B. A. Behrend's book on the *Ancien Regime* in pre-revolutionary France captured Schmokel's outlook very well: "...His belief in the virtues of bourgeois ideology, which indeed he does not see as an ideology at all but as the only correct way of looking at things." But Schmokel was by nature quite tolerant and easy-going, the opposite of an ideologue—probably a result, as in the case of Papa, of his experience with politics during the war. He didn't let our ideological differences get in the way of friendship and good relations.

The faculty member who made the greatest impression on me was the preeminent Holocaust scholar Raul Hilberg (1926-2007). Although I never had a chance to take a course from him, I heard him speak at several university functions. One that particularly sticks out in my mind was a panel discussion on the 100th anniversary of the Franco-Prussian War and the unification of Germany in the spring of 1971, in which Schmokel was also a panelist. Hilberg was a commanding presence. He spoke with the kind of authority that only comes from deep conviction and personal experience. His talk was mesmerizing, not so much because he had a way with words, but because he spoke from the soul.

The most enjoyable aspect of my return to graduate school was my exposure to books that I might never have read if they had not appeared on course syllabi. I was very impressed, for instance, by Erik Erickson's (1902-1994) *Young Man Luther* (1962), a book viewed by some historians as an unwarranted encroachment on their turf. Schmokel dismissed the whole genre of "psychohistory" as faddish and only marginally legitimate. "After all, you can't put dead historical figures on the couch." To me Erickson's book demonstrated how rewarding a psychoanalytical perspective could be. I loved Erickson's characterization of Luther's "secret furious inviolacy." Some of his insights were more banal, of course, but sound nonetheless: "Fathers, if they know how to hold and guide a child, function somewhat like guardians of the child's autonomous existence." One of his statements would have even more meaning for me a few years later, when I experienced the dissolution of our marriage: "Whatever ends in divorce loses all retrospective clarity because a divorce breaks the *Gestalt* of one love into the *Gestalten* of two hates." I recognized myself in the following rather uncomplimentary description of

Luther as "one of those addicts and servants of the word who never know what they are thinking until they hear themselves say it, and who never know how strongly they believe what they say until somebody objects...Hearing his own words had inspired his convictions." I could readily empathize with the following piece of advice: "Many individuals should not do the work they are doing, if they are doing it well at too great inner expense. Good work it may be in terms of efficiency; but it is also bad works." I recognized our own family dynamics in Erickson's analysis: "In truly significant matters people, and especially children, have a devastatingly clear, if mostly unconscious perception of what other people really mean, and sooner or later royally reward real love and take well-aimed revenge for implicit hate. Families in which each member is separated from the others by asbestos walls of verbal propriety, overt sweetness, cheap frankness, and rectitude tell one another off and talk back to each other with minute and unconscious displays of affect— not to mention physical complaints and bodily ailments—with which they worry, accuse, undermine, and murder one another."

Another book from which I learned a lot was Peter Pulzer's *The Origins of Political Anti-Semitism in Germany and Austria* (1964). It revealed to me how closely modern (and Christian) antisemitism were related to animosity against the emancipatory values of the left: equal and inalienable rights for all, democracy, internationalism, liberalism, socialism, secularism, indeed the whole set of social and political allegiances emanating from the Enlightenment and French Revolution. It also revealed to me how instrumentalized the charge of antisemitism had become after the founding of the state of Israel in 1948, when it was the left that was increasingly accused of antisemitism for standing up for Palestinian rights. It surely is one of the great ironies of history that today it is the Likud in Israel that represents the greatest political continuity of any governing party in the West with the ethnic nationalism of the far right before the Second World War.

Another book that made quite an impression on me was Ernst Nolte's *Three Faces of Fascism* (1963; English translation, 1967), the book that launched this former high school teacher's reputation as a historian and legitimated the notion of a generic fascism manifesting itself in varying forms in the 1920s and 1930s in every European nation with the exception of the Soviet Union. However, I instinctively questioned his judgment in identifying Friedrich Nietzsche as the progenitor of fascism. Only later, after Nolte's successive works documented Nolte's increasing shift to the right, did I realize that his derogatory interpretation of Nietzsche was a function of Nolte's efforts to exculpate the Christian conservatism that had been so instrumental in the fascists' rise to power all over Europe.

On June 8, 1971, Mama's sometime partner Connie Sherwin died of liver failure in the hospital in Newport. Mama had already moved out of Connie's house and back into her shack (and after the fire, into a trailer) on her own land, adjacent to Connie's farm, in April 1968. In June 1969 I commented on their feud:

> The Mama-Connie affair come full circle: eight years ago Connie was attracted to Mama because of the goat in her house, the unconventionality that freed [Connie] from her New Yorker dead end. Now she courts the approval of the townies by making fun of the goat in Mama's house.

Their relationship had undergone many ups and downs, and Connie was still hoping, shortly before the unexpectedly sudden end of her life, to persuade Mama to move back in with her. But Mama had a stubborn streak and rejected all invitations and inducements, even to the point of subsisting, for lack of money to buy food, on corn flakes in the winter of 1970-1971, as we found out after our return from Burlington at the end of the semester in May.

Trina with Cowie, Mama's trailer in the background,
and Minicucci's new house on the top of the hill

On June 9th I wrote in my journal:

> Last impressions of Connie: driving Mama home from the library [Mama volunteered as librarian in Albany] one day last year: Connie is walking up the hill toward [her neighbor] Roland Lawrence's. I slow down. She sees us, and, instead of ignoring us as expected, waves and makes a gesture as if to speak to us when we stopped. I ask Mama whether she wanted to stop. She says no, and I pick up speed as we go by. Shortly thereafter I vow to stop next time, no matter what Mama says, but there is no next time.

> We never were closer to Connie than at the time that Mama and she broke up. Steffi had already prepared an Easter present before we heard that Mama had moved out. Connie asked us, indirectly, to help persuade Mama to return. "What made her leave?" she asked. I said it probably was Connie's drinking. "But I've been drinking ever since she knows me." Shortly thereafter Mama successfully pressured us to break relations with Connie. "Talking badly about me is the passport to her house."

> Connie's inferiority to Mama; she was in the wrong because she was weaker.

Mama lost her voice (for about three weeks) from the moment she heard of Connie's death. "At five after eight Kate Davis drove up and said Connie had died at ten to eight," Mama reported. "I immediately went with Kate to call [Connie's brother] Bob, and when I got to the phone I had no voice."

Steffi attended the funeral a few days later, but I did not go. On June 13, I outlined what I thought would be a good plot for a novel:

> Story of Connie's funeral: Unable, despite the instructions she left, to prevent a ceremony at which Mama plays a leading part, sitting at graveside, in the "seats of honor," from which she would have been rudely dislodged if Connie were alive. Playing hostess afterwards in the house she deserted more than three years ago. Returning in triumph to live there and "run" the farm she was not permitted to run when Connie was alive. Will she permit Connie's cows on her land [a constant source of quarrels while Connie was alive]? Mama's main complaint

against Connie was that she went back on their original bargain—to farm together, using Connie's cows and barn, and Mama's land. It developed into a struggle for dominance, for who was to have the say-so. For Connie the need to play the "male role" was probably greatest. She wanted to take care of Mama, and certainly did for a time. Psychologically she was more dependent on Mama than Mama was on her. She behaved as she did to Mama, because she wanted to make Mama equally, or more, dependent on her. But she could not get Mama to return on her, Connie's, terms. The only thing that could make Mama come back was Connie's death. Now it is Mama who is taking care of Connie, or what's left of Connie. Mama suffered enough, no doubt, before reaping the harvest of her constancy. Her life is an object lesson on how to survive without worrying about it, or even trying very hard. To the superstitious it might seem that fate always rescues her just in the nick of time. And only last week I worried about the fact that the refrigerator which we procured for her (for a dollar at auction) had no shelves, and that with the hot weather her trailer would be invaded by the mosquitoes and black flies that find so many excellent breeding places in the vicinity!

A week later I commented on

Mama's defenselessness, it seemed, seeing her again for the first time after Connie's death. Aged in one way, yet more childlike in another way (there is no contradiction). For the first time I thought I could recognize what Connie must have found so attractive about her, that quality so entirely concealed behind a front of abusive anger and vituperation.

Steffi's refusal to look at Mama while she (Mama) was talking. This gesture, which I generally approve as a necessary method of retaining independence, surprised me now and brought me back to the reality of Mama's strength. I had expected Steffi to pity her.

Perhaps the grain of truth in Steffi's remark, when I asked her why she didn't want me to go to Connie's funeral, is what humiliated me so: "*Ich habe Angst du sagst etwas Peinliches zu Mama* (I'm afraid you'll say something embarrassing to Mama)."

Mama with Steffi on Mama's farm

Connie's brother, to whom Connie left the farm, asked Mama to run it until he could find a buyer. This meant that, ironically, several of our family get-togethers that summer were in Connie's house, where Mama had lived from 1964, after her first fire, until 1968. Mama now emphasized her cohesion with Connie, perhaps to remove the potential stigma of living in the house to which she had refused to return while Connie was alive. Her conversation was now sprinkled with, "*We* did this, *we* did that." Faithful not unto death, I thought, but after death. Gathering at Connie's house made me somewhat uncomfortable, not so much because it seemed a violation of Connie's memory, but rather because it acknowledged the power that Mama had to determine whether and when we were permitted to visit Connie's home.

Connie's death gave us four "children" the opportunity to pay off the mortgage on Mama's land, a right that Connie (who had taken out the mortgage in her own name with the bank in Orleans) had denied us in order to maintain Mama in a state of at least partial financial dependency even after Mama's steadfast refusal of Connie's repeated offers of financial support if Mama would return to her. After her death, Connie's brother was happy to be relieved of the monthly mortgage payments on Mama's land. In an effort to retain her financial independence Mama had previously sold about 25 choice acres of her property to "flatlanders" (the Minicuccis) from Connecticut, much to the dismay of us "children." The newcomers built a cabin in a very visible location on their newly acquired land for their family to visit during hunting season and vacations. To avoid having to sell off further parcels to support herself and pay the taxes, Mama decided to deed her property to her four children in return for the right to its use for the rest of her life. In the summer of 1972 Aunt Temple generously had a brand-new three-bedroom ranch house built for Mama on the farthest reaches of her property near the Black River, along with a small gambrel-roofed barn for her animals, mostly goats and sheep, with a hayloft on top. Aunt Temple's original intention was to reside with Mama in Vermont at least part of the year, but over the years her stays grew ever shorter as she sought to avoid any friction with Mama. Olaf, the only one of us without a foothold in Vermont at the time, subsequently bought out his chronically impecunious siblings as co-owners of Mama's property, and Aunt Temple deeded the house and the barn to him later as well. Olaf, in turn, took over the obligation for Mama's welfare. By paying off Mama's last outstanding contributions to qualify for social security (Mama had paid into the system in the late 1940s and early 1950s while working at the Briscoes and at various odd waitressing jobs) he enabled Mama to draw monthly social security checks at age 62 in 1974, thus assuring her a steady, if minimal, source of income that would make her economically independent, though not entirely self-sufficient, for the rest of her life. Olaf benefited as well by claiming her as a dependent on his income tax form and gaining possession of her 170 acre property with house and barn. "Olaf lets me play at farming," Mama told Maureen Dyer, a young admirer. "But you know, if I could do anything in the world, there's nothing I would rather be doing than farming." Farming was a way of life for Mama, perhaps a final tribute to the Bavarian peasant culture she had experienced during the war. "You go into farming," Mama said, "like you go into the theatre."

That summer Steffi and I again made the rounds of an ever-increasing number of crafts fairs, a practice we had begun in the summer of 1969 at an annual juried fair sponsored by a consortium of craftsmen in the picturesque town of Bennington in southern Vermont. The site of the fair shifted to Rhinebeck, New York, in the summer of 1971 to accommodate the growing number of exhibitors.

The new sign in front of our house

But the most lucrative fair, and one of the hardest to get into, was the one in Guilford, Connecticut, in the heart of one of the wealthiest residential areas in the country. Steffi and I had enjoyed what to us seemed like a spectacular success of several hundred dollars of sales in the summer of 1970. In succeeding years we sometimes doubled and even tripled those figures. The summer of 1971 was somewhat of a disappointment, however. This time I was to go alone so as to leave Steffi, who was pregnant (Nicky was born November 1st of that year), free to continue making jewelry at home. However, having arrived at Olaf's in Middletown, where he was once again teaching summer school at Wesleyan, I promptly came down with a nasty grippe. His 13-year-old son John, who had been slated to assist me, actually was left to run our booth entirely on his own. He did so very successfully, achieving a greater volume of sales than we had attained a year before.

The story had an interesting follow-up. Mama's staunchly conservative neighbor Roland Lawrence, Albany's representative to the state legislature notorious for his obstruction of any progressive social legislation, heard that something had gone wrong in Guilford. Whether because he credited me with greater strength than I had or because he refused to believe that I was capable of such a flagrant dereliction of duty, he got the story all wrong. When I returned to Vermont, he said, "Well, I heard that Steffi was sick down in Connecticut somewhere and John had to do all the selling for her." I set him straight on who it was that had gotten sick, but not without feeling that I had dropped a notch or two in his estimation. It was not the first time he made me feel deficient in meeting a personal test or obligation. On an earlier occasion, after one of Mama's cows had strayed on to his land (a not infrequent occurrence, given the state of Mama's improvised fences), he simply assumed that I would take care of this matter for her. "Do you want a rope around her nose to lead her?" he asked me, assuming as a matter of course that I knew when it was best to drive a cow or when it was best to lead her. Mama and he, on the other hand, despite their political and ideological differences, formed a mutual admiration society, admiring each other for the same trait: rugged individualism. "He wrings a respect for Republicanism from you," Mama said.

John Stackelberg, 1972

I had noticed some time ago that Mama's attitudes were often quite conservative, at least compared to mine. I thought, for instance, that her attitude toward American crimes in Vietnam was excessively forgiving (no doubt because they paled in comparison to the crimes she had witnessed in Germany during the Second World War), and I was shocked by her refusal to condemn with what I thought was appropriate harshness the young people involved in the nightrider attack on the Johnson home in the Irasburg Affair. Paradoxical as it may sound, Mama's conservatism was a function of her growing tolerance for all types of people, even the narrow minded and reactionary natives who were still well represented in the Northeast Kingdom in those days. She had the optimistic and progressive conviction that people were basically good, though she never hesitated to point out their corruptions and mistakes. Mama was a bit of a misanthrope, but the opposite of a cynic. She saw through sham and delusion clearly enough, but despite ritual exclamations of "it's hopeless" or "it's useless," she never gave in to pessimism or bitterness. Hence there was no contradiction between her penchant for personal and political criticism and her sometime acceptance of eccentric right-wing views. She did temper her apologetics for the Vietnam War in the 1970s, but her growing disenchantment with the war was often expressed rather indirectly, in such generic statements as, "I'm sick of war. It's the funniest thing. I can no longer read about war." Even Aunt Temple, who remained hawkish for a longer period and mocked me for my pacifist views, was beginning to change. "This war has lasted entirely too long," she conceded, though not yet quite ready to have it shortened by pulling out rather than by applying greater force. The publication in June of 1971 of the Pentagon Papers did much to legitimate the anti-war movement and led me to record the following observation in my journal: "Suddenly my article, calling for governments to act under the same rules and standards that govern the conduct of individual relations, doesn't seem so childish, silly, naïve anymore."

Mama's life may be said to have consisted of unfulfilled dreams, nicely captured (along with Mama's personal authority, her sense of humor, and her propensity to tease) by my sister Betsy in two vignettes she wrote in 1970 and subsequently sent to me:

> I was living in my mother's hand-made tarpaper shack [in 1966]. It was hard to keep it clean but one could manage it. All around the shack, however, was a tumble of mess and ruins from the old burned-down farmhouse. Wood lay all over, bricks, papers, it was not a pretty sight.

At times I was very depressed by my fate which had brought me to this pass. However, there were times without compare.

With Trina and Pferdi in front of our new Franklin stove, 1971

Every afternoon my mother came down [from Connie's house] to feed her animals and I always very formally asked her in for a cup of tea. My mother made a big point of not coming in unless she knocked, or I asked her in. She said: "Yes, put the water on, I'm dying of thirst." It was an extremely mild November afternoon and my mother suggested we drink our tea outdoors. We did. There we sat, behind us a tumble-down tarpaper shack and all around us a terrible mess.

Suddenly my mother said: "How do you like my rose garden?" Of course, I saw none, and I said so. "Why, I can see it plainly, the vines are only half-way up so far," my mother insisted and still I resisted. "All I can see is a terrible mess," I said with a certain vehemence. "Why Betsy, I can't understand that. I see that rose garden so very clearly, not only the flowers, but the steps that lead down to them, because it's a sunken garden. You do see that, don't you?" I was becoming infected as I knew I would, and I said, very reluctantly, "Yes, I am beginning to see your rose garden, Mama," and once converted, I became quite enthusiastic, and we added many details of perfection to the scene.

"And don't you love living in my mansion, Betsy? It's so spacious, three stories high with lots of extra rooms." For one minute I wanted to resist again and say, No, I don't like your tarpaper shack, but instead I really caught the fever and saw the beautiful house.

I don't live there anymore, but every time I go back to visit I see that lovely sunken garden in front of my mother's beautiful three-story white house.

*****

Yesterday [in 1970] I visited my mother, and it was another classic encounter.

As I was driving down she stood in the middle of the road to see who it was. When she recognized my car, she turned away, and I again felt that sinking feeling—Oh my God, she's in a bad mood. Well, I'll tell her I can only stay five minutes.

However, she recovered herself and before I had even stopped, she said: "How very opportune. I need you to stand in front of that pig who is trying to get out, while I get nails and a hammer." So, of course, I did. There I stood, waving a stick at a grunting pig, and thinking, you never know now, you never do.

That done, I said, could we take a small walk, and my mother jumped at the chance. Half way across the field I knew my dog was getting tired. I suggested we turn back, but no, my mother said we had hardly begun, and I knew we must continue.

We walked. Suddenly my mother stopped, looked all around her at the sloping valley and rolling hills and said: "This is my house." For one moment I was very startled, no house being visible, but then I said, "It's very lovely, you chose a beautiful spot."

"Yes, I like my houses to be protected." "I can certainly understand that," I said and wondered what would come next. It came:

"Oh well, you know," my mother said, "this is only one of my thirty houses."

I have pretty much given up resisting my mother and I said: "I didn't know, Mama. You must show me your other houses too." "Well, that would take at least five hours," my mother said in all seriousness.— "I guess we don't have time for that today then," I said.

"By the way, is this a two-story house?"

"Oh, I don't know," and with a sudden loss of interest we moved on.

My dog, Tamara, was very tired by now and I had to pick her up.

"Why not put her in your purse?" asked my mother. So I did. There sat Tamara, only her head looking out.

"She's not completely happy, but she'll settle," announced my mother. After that we walked in silence back to her trailer and I finished the visit with a cup of tea and two pieces of bread with honey."

In the spring of 1971, after two years of trying, Steffi finally got pregnant again. Our son Nicholas Olaf, named after my two brothers, was born on November 1st.

Nicky, November 1971

Steffi was sure he had been conceived on February 9th. "That was your birthday present to me," she said.

Trina nursing her Teddy

Dr. Gage, our chain-smoking local physician, had refused to preside over natural childbirth, which Steffi would have preferred. In those days fathers were not yet welcome in the delivery room, certainly not in Newport, Vermont. The baby was big and healthy and had what seemed to me a marvelously placid temperament. Trina accepted her sibling with a sense of pride, although she had hoped for a sister who would become her playmate.

Trina with her new brother

At the end of the fall semester I completed my MA thesis on the Irasburg Affair and at age 36 prepared to move on to the University of Massachusetts at Amherst for my PhD.

Trina with her Granny, Christmas 1971

4

AMHERST, MASSACHUSETTS, 1972-1974

My MA thesis on the *Irasburg Affair*, completed in December 1971, won the Vermont Bar Association Prize, but I never collected my $50 prize. By the time my degree came due in June 1972 I had already enrolled in a PhD program in history at the University of Massachusetts in Amherst. UMass was not my first choice, but by that time Harvard had learned from its past errors of judgment and refused to admit me to its graduate school for a third time. I could hardly have afforded it in any case. On the other hand, UMass not only offered me a teaching assistantship, but contrary to the usual practice allowed me to begin my studies in the spring semester. I rented a room in Amherst in January 1972, an easy three-hour drive from Irasburg down Interstate 91. Most weekends I returned to Irasburg, where Steffi was tending the new baby and five-year-old Trina while continuing to make jewelry and preparing to join me full-time in Amherst in the fall of 1972.

University of Vermont Professor Wolfe Schmokel had quite properly cautioned me against pursuing a PhD. The 1960s growth in the job prospects for fresh PhDs had come to an abrupt halt and gone into reverse. He thought I was making a big mistake to give up a secure position at Lake Region Union High School, especially with two young children to support. He warned me that I was quite likely to face unemployment on finishing my degree. Steffi, however, encouraged me to continue. We had no immediate financial worries, as I was a beneficiary of the GI bill, which in the mid-1960s had been extended to cover my years of military service. Steffi's flourishing jewelry business, to which I contributed by manning her booths at crafts fairs during the summers, even allowed us to save a little money and pay off the mortgage on our Irasburg home early.

Steffi's shop sign in the autumn

My favorite class at UMass in the spring of 1972 was Bob Griffith's course on post-World War Two U.S. history. Griffith, a 1967 PhD from the University of Wisconsin, had written an excellent book on Joseph McCarthy and very much shared the critical perspective on American Cold War policies of the new wave of younger American historians in the 1960s. His class was extremely lively with lots of open discussion and debate. Among my more interesting classmates was young Dennis McNally, who later wrote fascinating books on Jack Kerouac and on the Grateful Dead. He is today one of the leading authorities in the country on both those subjects. Griffith tried to get me to change my specialization to recent American history, but my mind was already made up, despite the fact that the German historian at UMass, Harold J. Gordon (who became my default advisor), adhered to the very opposite of my own political perspective. Gordon had recently published a book on *Hitler and the Beer Hall Putsch*, the obvious objective of which was to discredit the "New Left" and the sputtering, but still active student movement by drawing wholly unwarranted links to the right-wing Free Corps movement in Germany that had led to Hitler's failed putsch attempt in November 1923. Gordon went so far as to compare the civil rights march in Northern Ireland on "Bloody Sunday" in January 1972 (where thirteen marchers were killed by the British army) to Hitler's march on the *Feldherrnhalle* in Munich. Apparently to Gordon, all youthful or popular rebellions against constituted authority were the same. Knowing that he would not be able to avoid calling attention to the massive ideological differences between Hitler's movement and the American New Left, Gordon deliberately excluded all evidence from Hitler's 1924 trial from his book. Ironically, the book received a favorable review from the British medievalist Geoffrey Barraclough in the *New York Review of Books* for its challenge to the Whiggish liberal consensus on Nazism, which failed to adequately take the role of proletarian social forces into account. If Barrraclough had read the book closely, he would have realized that Gordon's dissent from the liberal consensus came not from the socially-oriented left but from the hard-core conservative right.

Gordon harbored an ill-concealed grievance against his *alma mater*, Yale, for having "banished" him to a second-tier university by neglecting to offer him a position on their faculty. He claimed that he would never get a position at an Ivy League school because he was brought up a Catholic. A colonel in the U.S. Army Reserve, Gordon admired the military caste, by no means excluding former German Wehrmacht officers, to whose post-war apologetics he gave rather too much credence. The villains in his narrative of the collapse of the Weimar Republic were the Social Democrats. When I asked him why he was so critical of the one party in Germany that best represented American values of civil liberties and democratic process, he claimed that it was the SPD that had undermined Weimar democracy by its excessive social welfare demands. Gordon had some more likeable eccentricities as well. He had a pet guinea pig who freely roamed around his library, forcing students whom he had summoned to tutorials at his home to keep a close watch over their papers while he lectured in a dreary monotone without notes, guided only by his deeply ingrained conservative biases. He brought his well-trained dog to his office, but sometimes it was difficult to tell whether his terse reprimands were addressed to his dog or to me. In my journal I recorded some of Gordon's idiosyncrasies and epigrams:

Gordon: "I don't like people who are holier than me."

My worst fears about Gordon, first raised by the warm acknowledgement that [UVM Professor] Schmokel gave him in his book, are confirmed. A rabid opponent of the "liberal left"—in this sense he is far to the right of Schmokel—he trembles with rage at the suggestion that Nazism had anything in common with conservatism. Suspecting that a book that I showed him—Reinhard Kühnl's *Die nationalsozialistische Linke*—might have taken this line, Gordon said: "I believe in the Sidney Painter way, to go to the primary sources first. If you read secondary sources first, you're likely to go to the sources with your mind already made up. I believe in the Yale system, reliance on primary sources. At Harvard they put more emphasis on *explication de texte*. The Harvard people are always telling me I don't use enough secondary sources." Very strait-laced students, usually recently discharged junior officers from the army, are attracted to Gordon and call him "sir." His positivistic approach actually makes a virtue of not taking ideas too seriously or going into them deeply; this is one course where a straightforward chronicle of events—with only a rudimentary explanation of causes—is not only acceptable, but desirable. One of his loyal students cautioned me, "Gordon likes papers that assume that the reader knows nothing about the subject." Gordon's autocratic manner appears deceptively informal, especially when he slings one leg over the side of his easy chair. His technique is more to ignore rather than subdue, although on occasion he will shout. He browbeats by monopolizing the conversation, in which he displays an undeniable virtuosity, smoothly shifting gears and direction by constantly qualifying what he says in a kind of free association. Taken as a whole his monologue is a mass of contradictions, but because of its spontaneity it appears to be entirely consistent—as indeed it is as a reflection of a closed ideology. When he speaks, he leans back *genussvoll* (with pleasure), and closes his eyes...

Gordon held back by his own prejudices so much that he won't even read Peter Gay's book on Weimar culture (subtitled, *The Outsider as Insider*

[1968]), although Peter Gay's interpretation is colored by the same anti-student-movement bias as Gordon himself subscribes to. Probably Gay's previous books in defense of Rousseau and the Enlightenment have put Gordon off...

Gordon: "I'm for law and order, although I do think our laws are for the most part no good and we'd probably do best to start over again from scratch..."

Gordon: "Hitler was just as moralistic as Martin Luther King."

Gordon's study: shelves of books framing a glass-enclosed collection of hand-guns. The cobwebbed quality of his study. It could be *gemütlich*, it should be *gemütlich*, but it is cold, lifeless: everything is dusty and superannuated. It is institutionalized disorder. Things have been lying in the same state of disarray for decades. It reeks of unwillingness to change.

Gordon's worst moment came in a seminar he conducted with the well-known Russian specialist and chair of the history department at UMass, Robert H. McNeal (1930-1988), who was killed a few years later in a tragic automobile accident. Somehow it came out that I could trace my ancestry to the Baltic-German nobility. Gordon blurted out that the Baltic-German nobility were heavily intermarried with Jews. No doubt he meant this as an explanation of my perversely left-wing views, but I was very pleased. Unintentionally he had exposed his antisemitic bias for all to hear. One of my fellow-students told me later that he had been quite shocked, and even Professor McNeal later apologized for Gordon's uncalled-for remark.

Gordon's teaching assistant Michael Barrett, today a respected military historian at The Citadel, gave me what I thought was a telling example of Gordon's problematic influence on his students, as described in my journal on 26 November 1972:

How history gets distorted: Michael Barrett planning to ask his class whether they think the narrator of *All Quiet on the Western Front*, disillusioned with the war, might not have made a highly likely candidate for Nazism. Far more serious than his erroneous assumption that the narrator actually returned from the war is his failure to appreciate the incongruity between the narrator's values and the values of Nazism. The extent of his misunderstanding: he claims that, after all, the narrator, who was disgusted by the patriotic tub-thumping and the beer-hall strategy with which he was confronted while on leave in his home town, therefore also [like the Nazis] believed in a stab in the back on the part of civilians!

As my advisor and the only Germanist in the history department, Gordon could not be excluded from my oral exam or dissertation committees. Fortunately, I could balance his influence with much more congenial members of the department. I chose as my dissertation supervisor the young intellectual historian William M. Johnston, who had graduated from Harvard College two years after me and had already completed his PhD under Crane Brinton in the mid-1960s. Through Johnston I received what I called "my second Harvard education." Johnston was conservative and anti-Marxist as well, but he was much more open to critical opinion than Gordon and was genuinely fascinated by ideas and ideologies of all kinds. Unlike Gordon, Johnston's conservatism reflected the "ethos of scholarship," a renunciation of all activism and presentism in favor of disinterested investigation and explanation. One of Johnston's most endearing traits was his appreciation of defenders of lost causes, the tragic view of life he found best represented in the European rather than the American intellectual tradition. He had just published a massive tome, *The Austrian Mind: An Intellectual and Social History*, which was, however, panned by the eminent historian Carl Schorske in *The American Historical Review* for allegedly neglecting the social context of the ideas and the authors he discussed. Johnston was an excellent teacher, generating enthusiasm for his discipline of intellectual history while maintaining strict academic standards, encouraging open debate, and allowing students to pursue specific interests of their own. In my journal I noted "Johnston's effect of making me suddenly doubt things I say, things I have said before with perfect confidence. His effect of making me aware of my contradictions and inaccuracies."

Johnston at his best, conveying an excitement about Hegel and the Hegelian dialectic, which far from being exclusive and rigid, will always want to embrace and understand the other side. Johnston is a better teacher than he is a writer. He is especially good in refusing to be caught in sophistries and technicalities, at going to the heart of the matter. I find myself (sometimes deliberately) imitating his expression when listening intently, mouth barely open, lower lip slightly drawn in, eyes focused in midair.

His course on European intellectual history in academic year 1972-1973 remains one of my fondest memories of my time at UMass. From Johnston I also picked up the habit of very close reading of student papers, a practice for which I later gained a positive reputation at Gonzaga University. Students appreciated my very specific stylistic and substantive suggestions, which they found much more helpful than vague comments such as "awkward" or "unclear" or "needs revision." Gordon, by contrast, used a rack of ready-made stamps—"VAGUE," "HOW?" "WHY?" and so on—to speed his correction of student papers.

The third member of my dissertation committee was Miriam Usher Chrisman (1920-2008), a pioneering scholar of the German Reformation in Strasbourg in the sixteenth century. Having done most of her research in the formerly German province of Alsace, she could corroborate for me that my study of the Alsatian dramatist and publicist Friedrich Lienhard (1865-1929) accurately reflected the *völkisch* ideology so prevalent in Germany's contested border regions in Imperial Germany before and during (and even more so after) the First World War. She gave me encouragement and a sense of achievement; she said that writing her dissertation had been much harder than giving birth to her children. Mrs. Chrisman, as she was called at UMass, had a famous father, also a professor, who once invited a theologian to their house to explain the Trinity to her. She suffered from asthma, which did not affect her when she was speaking, but came to the fore when she was forced to listen to rambling students in class. Her one rather unpleasant trait was talking tough out of the side of her mouth—the product, I thought, of her pre-women's liberation years in a masculine world.

Lienhard was one of three protagonists of my dissertation on *völkisch* ideology; the other two were a devoted, but short-lived Wagnerian, Heinrich von Stein (1857-1887) and the influential racial theorist Houston Stewart Chamberlain (1855-1927), through whose biography I could establish links between nineteenth-century *völkisch* ideology and National Socialism. My model was Fritz Stern's pioneering work on *The Politics of Cultural Despair*, a study of three prominent German nationalist writers, Paul de Lagarde (1827-1891), Julius Langbehn (1851-1907), and Arthur Möller van den Bruck

(1876-1925), which first appeared in 1963. Reflecting the affirmative culture of 1950s America, Stern targeted what he considered to be radical outsiders and negativistic prophets of doom who believed that Western civilization was on the path to ruin. Hence the famous title of his book, which added a new phrase to the vocabulary of historians of the German Empire. Influenced by the radical countercurrents of the 1960s, I was more concerned to show how very much part of the monarchist mainstream *völkisch* ideologists actually had been. After substantial revisions, my dissertation was eventually published as *Idealism Debased: From Völkisch Ideology to National Socialism* in 1981.

As a student at the University of Massachusetts in 1973

My closest friend at UMass was a young German exchange student from Freiburg University, Andreas Kunz. He was married to a woman of Lebanese extraction, the daughter of a restaurant-owner in St. Johnsbury, Vermont, less than an hour from our home in Irasburg. Hence we saw quite a bit of each other both in class and outside the classroom setting. Although Andy was thirteen years younger than I was, politically we saw pretty much eye-to-eye. Heavily influenced by the radical German student movement, he still had strong Marxist sympathies in those days. This did not make it easier for him to get along with Johnston, who called him a "self-hating German." Johnston did, however, agree with my rejoinder, which was, "Better than his elders!" Although Johnston was open-minded and fascinated by all ideas—even those of Marx—he was put off by what he claimed was the "reflex reaction" of Marxists. His real beef against Marx was that he made metaphysics irrelevant, the realm in which Johnston felt most at home. Johnston could not abide the notion that religion and metaphysics were mere "superstructures," forever doomed to be determined by the "economic base." Andy would later go on to earn his PhD at Berkeley under the preeminent economic historian Gerald Feldman (1937-2007) with a dissertation on the German civil service in the 1920s. This was Andy's stepping stone to a brilliant academic career in Germany at the Institute for European Studies in Mainz. Just when Andy lost his left-wing orientation I can't say, but I do remember his telling me, at the time of German reunification in 1990, that there would be no room in Germany for any party to the left of the SPD. I tried to contradict him, but he brushed my objections aside. Today *Die Linke*, the Left Party, is very much alive, though bearing little resemblance to its East German communist predecessor, the SED (Socialist Unity Party).

In August 1972 Tempy had a life-threatening auto-accident in France, where he had been working for the brokerage firm Kidder, Peabody for several years. He had to have his damaged spleen removed, but otherwise made a remarkably rapid and successful recovery. In my journal I recorded a letter from him,

> fully retaining his objective, descriptive eye despite the battering his body took in the accident. Sign of health: the only lesson he seems to have derived from the accident is, fasten your seatbelts. Because he now believes in this, he has become, in his words, "less of a cynic." He calls his present hospitalization "without doubt the longest period of wasted time" in his life and frets to get back to Kidder Peabody where things are currently in unrest because a key figure has just quit.

Tempy enjoyed his work, even though he disarmingly confessed to me, "I'd like to make a lot of money, but I don't know just how." In the event he never made the millions he was hoping for, but he retained his sense of humor and imperturbable disposition. Tempy and I did not agree on political matters, especially when, after his transfer to the London office of Kidder, Peabody, where he spent most of his career, he defended Margaret Thatcher's union-busting policies. To me it seemed that his increasingly conservative views confirmed Marx's notion that people's ideas were usually determined by the way they made their living (being determines consciousness, and not vice-versa). My son Nick visited Tempy at his new home in England in the early 1990s and was taken aback by Tempy's instant assumption that he, Nick, shared my left-wing views. A good example of how sons (or daughters) are sometimes doomed to pay the price for their fathers' sins.

Mama was idolized by many of the local "hippies", part of a growing cohort of 1960s drop-outs who had settled in little communal pockets throughout rural Vermont in the early 1970s. The "hippies" admired her for her embodiment of agrarian self-sufficiency, having turned her back on "chasing the almighty dollar" and living quite contentedly, though austerely, off the land. Her favorite readings were *The Rural New Yorker* and a journal on the raising of goats. In 1973 Mama was actually featured on the cover of *Yankee Magazine* as a model practitioner of a newly popular rural lifestyle.

Mama on the cover of *Yankee Magazine*, 1973

Some of Mama's "hippie" friends earned some money working with the local construction crew on the home and barn that Aunt Temple was building for Mama on Mama's property that summer of 1972.

1972 was also the most frustrating election year of my long life, the disappointment greater even than it would be in 1980 or in the year 2000. Senator George McGovern of South Dakota had won the Democratic nomination for President, raising hopes not only for an end to the war in Vietnam, where American involvement was winding down under public pressure in any case, but for a true break with the imperialistic foreign policy that the United States had pursued since the end of the Second World War. On 25 October 1972 I recorded in my journal my sense of helplessness in preventing Nixon's reelection:

> The peculiar satisfaction and strength I got from the blazing NIXON-AGNEW bumper sticker on a shiny huge new car of one of Steffi's customers at her Open House. A guest of [our neighbor] Yvette's had rather provocatively parked her car to block the driveway. When I went over to ask the guest to move, I knew it would be unpleasant. The sticker on Steffi's customer's car made me feel more sure of myself and my rights—though I regretted feeling so, for it just proves how unbeatable they are this year.

> Who has not felt the inevitability of certain events—despite the fact that you can see what's coming in the future? The absolute hopelessness of turning things around. The realization that only bitter experience will be able to provide a corrective. It is then that one can share, if not Kissinger's contempt for intellectuals, at least his conviction that they are not important. Only, where he is glad, I am sorry.

Even news of the break-in at the headquarters of the Democratic National Committee in the Watergate complex in June 1972 could not prevent Nixon's landslide reelection in November. Nixon used the opportunity to once again escalate the war in the so-called "Christmas bombing" of Hanoi in December. I followed the news on CBS:

> Walter Cronkite choking on the irony of Nixon's annual physical check-up, in which he was pronounced in excellent physical shape, except

that he did not get enough exercise! And this while the heaviest bombardment in the history of aerial warfare rained down on Vietnam. Eric Sevareid running scared (of the Administration's campaign to get locally affiliated stations to reject the national network's "ideological plugola"): formulating his criticisms in language no one can understand who isn't already familiar with what he's talking about.

Mama, who had preferred Eugene McCarthy to Robert Kennedy in the run-up to the 1968 election, but was now firmly in the McGovern camp, compared the public mood to the mood in Germany during the war: even those persons quite opposed to Nazism felt they had no choice but to support them to the hilt in the war to prevent the destruction of their country. She thought the same dynamic might be at work in this country, except that Americans did not risk destruction of their country, only a "loss of prestige."

The United States finally agreed to stop fighting in Vietnam on 27 January 1973. I had no illusions that the end of active American participation in the war would heal the divisions at home. On January 26th I wrote:

> The quite misplaced confidence that the end of the Vietnam War will end divisions at home based on the misunderstanding that the division was caused by the war. But the division was part of the war: it continues even after the fighting has stopped, even if it is temporarily repressed by the energy which the dominant power can now bring to bear against the "enemy" at home.

It was the Watergate scandal that finally brought an end to the Nixon presidency in 1974 and the subsequent end of the Vietnam War in 1975 (two years after the peace accords, which Nixon had ignored by ordering the secret bombing of Laos and Cambodia). Incriminating details about the Administration's direct involvement in the break-in, and later the cover-up, trickled out at regular intervals beginning in January 1973. The Administration had successfully prevailed on the burglars to plead guilty to avoid a potentially damaging trial, but two young *Washington Post* investigative reporters, Bob Woodward and Carl Bernstein, discovered that the burglars had been paid off to keep quiet from a secret slush fund under the control of the White House. Woodward and Bernstein had been alerted to the fund's existence by an FBI agent known only as "Deep Throat", who told the reporters to "follow the money." His identity was not revealed until after his death in the 1990s. For its enterprising investigative journalism, the *Post* would receive the Pulitzer Prize. Top presidential advisers Bob Haldeman and John Ehrlichman were forced to quit in April, and in May a special Senate committee under Senator Sam Ervin was convened to investigate the cover-up. The committee hearings led to the disclosure of one incriminating fact after another. Nixon sought to avert the inevitable by firing the special prosecutor in the case, Archibald Cox (1912-2004), who had insisted that the White House turn over crucial incriminating audiotapes of the President's discussions of the case. The incident became known as the "Saturday Night Massacre" when both Attorney General Elliott Richardson and his Deputy William D. Ruckelshouse resigned to avoid having to carry out the President's order to fire Cox. In 1974 Nixon finally lost his hold on power. In July the Supreme Court ruled 8-0 that the President must turn over his tape recordings to the Watergate prosecutor. The House Judiciary Committee under Peter Rodino (1909-2005) voted 27-11 to recommend impeachment for the President's role in the Watergate conspiracy, and in early August, seeing the handwriting on the wall, Nixon became the first President in American history to resign his office.

This was an exhilarating period for me, in retrospect two of the happiest years of my life. The disintegration of the Nixon Administration, with its odious personnel and policies, was exciting to behold. The judicial system functioned as it was meant to, enforcing the law without distinction as to rank or status, and the constitutional conflict between the legislative and executive branches of government ended with a victory of the former, as indeed the Constitution had prescribed. A tragic exception to the generally up-beat development of events in 1973-1974 was the tragic news of the CIA-supported military coup in Chile on 9/11/73. The brutal killing of Salvador Allende (1908-1973) led me to record in my journal "the same sickening feeling as at the death of Kennedy, and the [Soviet] invasion of Czechoslovakia in August 1968." In early 1974 the expulsion of Aleksandr Solzhenitsyn (1918-2008) from the Soviet Union left me with very mixed feelings. On the one hand it seemed to show the bankruptcy of a communist system that could tolerate no dissent. On the other hand, I was disgusted by the efforts of right-wingers to exploit his expulsion to revive an anti-communist (and anti-Marxist) crusade, based on the totally mistaken claim that Solzhenitsyn was a representative of Western democratic ideas. He soon proved to be as critical of Western democracy as he had been of that other "Western" import into Russia, Marxism. In my journal I wrote, "Why Solzhenitsyn had to go: it is easier to subvert a system based on cooperation (the USSR at least in theory), than one based on competition (the U. S.)."

In search of a college-level teaching position at a time of severely declining job opportunities, I attended the annual conference of the American Historical Association (AHA) in San Francisco in December 1973. On transcontinental flights most airlines still furnished the upper deck of the huge Boeing 747s as a lounge open to all passengers, and I remember a delightful flight, sipping cocktails on comfortable couches and conversing with members of the UMass history faculty heading to the same destination. I stayed with my young "godson" Johnnie Van Duyl at his place near Berkeley, commuting by BART to the conference every day. I had only one pre-scheduled job interview, with a committee from San Diego State University that was looking for a combination of specializations in Modern Germany and European Intellectual History. As one of perhaps fifty or sixty candidates being interviewed for this job at the conference, I didn't think I had much of a chance. However, to my great delight, some months later I was offered the position. I attributed my success to two factors: Having been told that the retiring professor I would be replacing was hard of hearing, I made every effort to speak as loudly and clearly as I could. More importantly—as I was later told by the chairman of the committee—I was the only candidate who had a clear idea of how he would organize a nineteenth-century European intellectual history course. Interested as I was in political ideas, or in the political consequences of ideas, I said I would use the French Revolutionary tradition as my organizing principle, tracking support for or opposition to this tradition in various European countries and analyzing intellectual movements in their relationship to this tradition. I envisioned a course in which I could juxtapose the French and German political and intellectual traditions, a framework in which I could readily draw on my dissertation research on *völkisch* ideology. The fact that the Latin American specialist Lewis Hanke (1905-1993) of the UMass history faculty was the president-elect of the AHA in 1974 didn't hurt my chances of successfully competing with PhDs from much more prestigious universities, either!

I spent the academic year 1973-1974 writing my dissertation on Stein, Lienhard, and Chamberlain. Chamberlain was the most interesting and most important writer of the three. The unifying theme was the evolution of *völkisch* ideology from an apparently innocuous and high-minded anti-commercial aesthetic doctrine (Wagnerism) to a virulently racist and anti-democratic ideology (National Socialism) in the span of half a century, in which the trauma of the First World War was, of course, the main catalyst in the transition. The topic involved a thorough study of antisemitism, probably the most distinctive marker of German *völkisch* thought. The one consistent theme, I concluded, in all historical forms of antisemitism, from theological and Christian anti-Judaism to the lethal modern economic, political, and racial varieties, was the conviction that Jews were inherently selfish and "immoral," refusing to accept the prevailing Christian religious creed or to conform to the conventional dictates of gentile society. If the political right stood for received tradition and existing arrangements in all areas of life, it was virtually inevitable that antisemitism would become a major ingredient in right-wing thought, and Jews the major scapegoats for all the disruptive changes that modernization, commercialization, democratization, industrialization, secularization, and urbanization entailed. The fateful radicalization of the antisemitic movement in Germany occurred in my view in 1920, not only because of the consolidation of Hitler's leadership of the fledgling Nazi Party in that year, but because of the different reactions of the youthful leaders of the Nazi Party and their older conservative counterparts to the failure of the "Kapp Putsch" to overthrow the Weimar Republic in March 1920. The Nazis and their extremist allies attributed the failure of the coup precisely to the willingness of more mainstream conservative nationalists to cooperate with those few Jews who shared their conservative and German nationalist ideology and supported a military dictatorship. The Nazis came to the fateful conclusion that their project of destroying the Republic and its democratic institutions—a necessary precondition in their view for reversing the results of the First World War and preparing for a renewed war of aggression—could only succeed if all cooperation with Jews, whether "conservative" or not, were suspended. The categorical extrusion of Jews from Germany (and eventually Europe) became in their view the indispensable prerequisite for German expansion.

As it happened, my intensive study of antisemitism coincided with the so-called Yom Kippur war in October 1973, which, after initial setbacks resulting from the surprise factor, turned into another decisive Israeli military triumph. The unquestioning American and European support for Israel brought into focus the peculiar symbiosis between Zionism and European antisemitism I had already discovered in the *völkisch* writers I had been studying (but surprisingly also in the works of Theodor Herzl [1860-1904], one of the pioneers of Zionism). On 20 October I tried to put this counter-intuitive notion of a symbiosis between apparently conflicting ideologies into words in my journal:

> The connection between anti-Semitism and support for Israel: Israel is seen both as a convenient receptacle for the "excess" number of Jews in other countries of the world, and, more important, as a vehicle for instilling in Jews the "positive" values of nationalism and militarism. At the very least, support for Israel is seen as an effective way of defusing Jewish skepticism, pacifism, and social radicalism. At its worst it serves as a cover for anti-Semitism at home, and the whole complex of anti-intellectualism that accompanies it.

Although the fundamentalist Christian Zionism of the radical religious right was not yet the powerful political force it was destined to become at the end of the century and the beginning of the twenty-first century, the dynamic at work in the growth of this malignant reactionary movement was already clearly discernible.

The Yom Kippur War provoked a retaliatory boycott on oil exports by the oil-producing nations of the Middle East and led, temporarily, to long lines at gas stations here in the U. S. and Europe. Mama "loves the energy crisis," as our cousin Ginny Biddle put it, which seemed to validate Mama's own decision to give up driving a year or two before. She was impelled to this decision not only by the expense of maintaining a car, but also by her failing eyesight, which sometimes forced her to enlist the aid of her passenger(s) to determine whether the car she saw in the distance was coming toward us or going our way. Unbeknownst to us at the time, the oil crisis marked a turning point in American economic fortunes, launching a period of "stagflation" that lasted well into the 1980s, and a redistribution of wealth upwards to the highest income groups that is still continuing today. However, the price of gas was still very inexpensive in the U. S. In 1974 our cross-country trip in our new Volkswagen bus to our new destination in San Diego cost us only a little over $100 in fuel.

I finished my dissertation in the spring of 1974. Steffi took the children on a trip to Germany to visit her mother and father in April, allowing me to devote every waking moment to the completion of this project. On April 5th I noted two "overlapping ambivalences" in the motivations I brought to my dissertation:

> One, wanting not to fall into the trap of just joining the winning side and ritualistically condemning Chamberlain and Lienhard as precursors of National Socialism: wanting to show, in other words, the persuasive side of National Socialism. Secondly, wanting to condemn as strongly as I can similar nationalistic forces on the American scene in the present. How to accomplish both?? I call these purposes ambivalent, because each serves to weaken the other.

In the end I was dissatisfied with the final product not because of the content, but because of its sloppy appearance. Trying to save the cost of a professional typist, I typed the entire manuscript myself on my old portable typewriter. The final copy was marred not only by the inadequacies of my superannuated machine, but also (as I later discovered) by the numerous typographical errors caused by my excessive haste just to get the damn thing done!

5

San Diego, 1974-1976

We packed up our VW bus and left Vermont on 12 August 1974 on the first of what would turn out to be at least a dozen transcontinental trips, as every year we kept returning to Vermont for the summer until our final parting in 1982. Our first stop in 1974 was in Utica, New York. I began a travelogue at our next stop in Akron, Ohio, the following day:

> Two trucks, battling for the lead, at a snail's pace on a long hill, hogging both lanes. The traffic builds up behind. I am behind the truck in the passing lane. Someone in a great hurry pulls into the right-hand lane, betting that the truck in his lane will win out. The lead changes several times. In the end, after a good ten minutes, the truck in my lane wins out. The car next to me cuts in ahead of me from the right and spurts past. We have dropped back into the right-hand lane, nonplussed and a little scared by this naked display of competition. Car upon car with Ohio plates pass us, as if used to such goings-on on the highway. Only a woman in the passenger seat, passing close to my left, shakes her head very slowly with closed lips while staring straight ahead—as if to reassure me that not all Ohioans had become inured to such highway dramatics.

> Unable to get a room at the Holiday Inn at Akron because most rooms were reserved for a convention. A charter bus of convention-goers was just arriving, neck-tied and well-fed. Steffi was disappointed. *"Ich wollte*

schon immer da bleiben wo die Welt sich trifft (I always wanted to stay where the world meets)."

August 14, Effingham, Illinois. Sign on the window of a car from Pennsylvania passing us: "Hang on—San Diego". "I wanted to put a sign in our window, too," Steffi said.

August 15, Joplin, Missouri. Memories of my first over-night stay in Joplin, in my Olds on a cold night in March 1958. Memories, too, of Route 66 out of St. Louis to Fort Leonard Wood. Much of it has now been converted into Interstate 44, killing off most of the old businesses en route in the process.

Trini selecting a postcard of a Marion pony to send to Juliet (she bought it in an Indiana county famous for its ponies). Steffi chided her for always selecting a card with a subject that interested her rather than the person for whom the card was intended. Trini took this reproach to heart at the Meramec Caves in Stanton, Mo., and selected a picture of a stalactite that resembled a statue of the Virgin Mary. "Alexi likes the Virgin Mary," she explained.

The Meramec Caves a disappointment. Not because they weren't worth seeing, but because of the trappings: gaudy lights, hyperboles, and sensation-pandering. The presentations diminished the natural sights, as if they were worth seeing only because famous people had viewed them: Art Linkletter's use of a nook in the cave for a honeymoon room on his practical joke show, "People are funny," was billed as a main attraction, and as a climax an American flag was projected onto a wall of onyx stalactite, reenacting the dedication of that part of the cave to those who had fallen in World War II.

August 16, Clinton, Oklahoma. Ran into 110 degree heat in southwestern Oklahoma and turned in early. Trini spent two hours in the pool and learned by herself what I had been trying to teach her, without success, all summer: to dog-paddle. Now the temperature is 97 degrees and seems cool. "If it would only stay that way," Steffi says.

August 17, Albuquerque. The heat yesterday as scary as the severe cold in Vermont. The fear that it would never cool off again, and that we would have to crawl to San Diego in short, frantic laps.

Steffi, on seeing the Coca-Cola advertisements of American scenery: "Why do we never go by these scenes?"

August 18, Flagstaff, Arizona. On the road: a small roadside chapel, a wood-frame building the size of a chicken-coop, at a rest-area on Interstate 40 west of Gallup, New Mexico. A sign to get travelers to stop: "Relax and Reflect."

In a café, Winslow, Arizona. Ill feeling toward what appeared to be a typically boisterous redneck, cracking crude jokes partly with, partly at the expense of the waitress—but relieved of my distaste by the discovery that one of his companions was what appeared to be a full-blooded Indian.

The coolest, most pleasant weather of the trip in—Arizona!

Shortness of breath and chest pangs yesterday and today: worries greatly diminished by a sign at Holbrook, AZ: elevation 5,000 feet. Flagstaff is 7,000 feet: the first night without an air-conditioner.

August 19, Yuma, Arizona. Not quite believing Bill Mitchell [a fellow grad-student at UMass] when he told me of making much better mileage at high elevations: thinking this was one more of those little exaggerations that everyone makes. Greatly surprised, however, to make better than 25 miles per gallon between Albuquerque and Holbrook after averaging only 19 to 20 miles per gallon before.

The heat so intense between Phoenix and Yuma that one longed to remain completely motionless—to avoid the *heat* factor of the wind.

August 20, San Diego. Thoughts on driving through the desert: Vermont is lovely; California is magnificent.

Not all of my impressions of San Diego were positive, however. I was put off by a large sign raised high in front of a Presbyterian church: "If God were permissive, He would have given us the ten suggestions." The "educational" TV station identified itself with a salute to "San Diego, America's finest city." I soon noted a predilection for using the term "world-record" as a descriptive qualifier, whether it was of a marathon, a volleyball tournament, or a banjo-playing contest.

We settled into the home on 5358 Saxon Street of a colleague on leave, Bob Filner, who would later be elected to Congress for many terms as one of the more progressive representatives from southern California. My appointment was temporary, a one-year contract, with some prospects of renewal, but very little likelihood of conversion to the tenure track (despite the hope I was given of this possibility at my AHA interview). With an over-sized history department of forty-two members, San Diego State University was in retrenchment mode, and concern about my job dogged me for the entire year until my contract was finally renewed for one more year in the spring. In my journal I noted the irony that I had felt more confident about getting a teaching position last year—although I had not yet begun writing my dissertation!

In retrospect, I made a serious error of judgment in dragging my heels in joining the faculty union. My salary was only $14,000, and I could hardly afford the considerable annual dues, especially with the likelihood of the termination of my contract at the end of the year. But I had another, less defensible reason for rejecting the requests of my colleagues, who wanted 100 percent departmental membership to strengthen the union in its negotiations with the administration. My insecure status had made me quite critical of the tenure system, which at this early stage of my career seemed to me less a vehicle to job security than an obstacle to getting a job. Elimination of tenure would open up many more positions to competition based (at least in theory) solely on merit; in a fair contest I selfishly believed I had an excellent chance to prevail. My fellow one-year appointee, John Cumbler, a labor historian who succeeded in getting a job at the University of Louisville for the following academic year, tried to convince me that collegial solidarity would ultimately be of much greater benefit to me than going it alone. How right he was became clear to me in spring 1976 when the department, forced to cut back by a dean who rejected all "decisions of the heart," voted by a narrow margin to eliminate my position. The Russian specialist in the department, Neil Heyman, offered to take over my upper-division courses. Henceforth SDSU would no longer have a specialist in German and European intellectual history.

I did not help my cause, either, when at a departmental meeting on 3 October 1975 I found myself casting what turned out to be the swing vote—and I was on the conservative side!

The issue was whether a Native-American history course, taught by Native-American Studies personnel as a course in the history department, should be permitted to continue teaching the course in the department despite very critical student evaluations. The curriculum committee (with traditionalists Jon Sutherland, Raymond Starr, and Dennis Berge) recommended that the course not be offered next semester in order to give the Native-American staff a chance to iron out the flaws in the course. The course would then continue in the fall with the participation of a history department member (probably Berge, who claimed not to have enough time to participate in the coming spring semester). But a sizable group in the department felt that this was another case of the white man telling the redskins what to do and pleaded for a continuation of the course in the spring. A motion to that effect was made. It was amended to read that the course be given, provided the course was revised to the satisfaction of the department and a member of the department participate in its planning. I supported the amendment, which passed, but opposed the motion, which failed—by one vote.

When I got out of the meeting I had pangs of conscience. Why, when I had the chance, had I not stood by the liberal forces? After all, Ray Starr's arguments that the syllabus was lacking in organization and that the teacher of the course couldn't say whether he was teaching a course in Indian history or in Indian-White relations were extremely flimsy and only reflected Starr's prejudices about what constituted a good course. The reason probably was that I did not like the downgrading of student evaluations that the liberal motion implied. After all, my good evaluations were the strongest thing I had going for me in my quest for a job. If they were to be dismissed as unimportant, my position was weakened. I could rationalize my vote against the motion on other grounds as well: Dave Weber (1940-2010), who supported the motion, had suggested that it might be best to just let the curriculum committee handle the matter rather than jeopardize good relations by having the whole department come down on the course. But the amendment to the motion had precisely this effect and would in any case have prevented the course from being offered in the spring. My sense of guilt, however, resulted from the realization that this was just a rationalization. In the crunch I had come down in favor of traditional attitudes intolerant of failure, because, at the moment, or so it seemed, I stood to gain from such attitudes. Whether I really stand to gain is very questionable. The people who initiated the motion to retain me last year all came from the liberal camp. Raymond Starr would vote against me anyway—good evaluations or not—because he accepted the conservative administrators' arguments that the department was too big, etc., and the more I reflected on the meeting, the more I recognized the necessity of opposing the exclusivist, authoritarian mentality embodied in the curriculum committee's treatment of the Native-American course: the presumption of "white fathers" running the department along the rigid lines that places their own rigidity in a favorable light, because it sanctifies rigidity as the educational *summmum bonum*. In the long run that attitude is far more damaging to me than any failure to heed teaching evaluations. One has to be consistent in one's support of democracy and experimentation.

I recalled Steffi's warning the previous year not to trust Raymond Starr: "*Trau dem Raymond nicht. Er ist schadenfroh.*" And indeed his was the only dissenting vote (as I was told by Bob Filner, back from his sabbatical) when the department voted almost unanimously in December 1975 to request an extension of my contract for a third year, a request that the administration denied. Filner and I had something else in common, besides our distrust of Raymond Starr. Bob was fighting for tenure while I was fighting for a job. I admired his chutzpah in making no concessions to the conservative forces despite his precarious position. He entitled his colloquium talk "Sex, Science, and Society," starting his talk by saying, "I don't know if it's science screwing politics, or the other way round, but that's where the sex comes in."

Students were my strongest supporters in my quest to remain at SDSU. One of my best friends was a very intelligent student, son of a Jewish father ("a rich Florida merchant by the name of Solomon") and a non-Jewish mother, whose maiden name he adopted. He had been brought up by a rigid, anti-intellectual step-father by the name of Shultz, who resented his step-son's bookishness. Though obviously drawn to his Jewish background as a potential source of strength and belonging, my student proclaimed himself an agnostic—which made it easy and comfortable for me to get along with him. In my journal I noted the following observation:

> Steve's attitude toward his Jewish background like my attitude toward my aristocratic background: proud of it, but unable to fully identify with it—and to some degree therefore turning against it.

Steve acknowledged a weakness, his attraction to "powerful intellects:"

> Walking by a classroom in which Charlie Hamilton [a recent acquisition from the University of Chicago] was teaching, the word "transubstantiation" on the blackboard caught his eye. He stopped and looked in: "I've got to sit in on one of his lectures some time." It was something of a let-down for him to be told that I had left the writing on the board in the class preceding.

My student went on to a remarkable career. He earned his PhD at Oxford University with a specialization in the French Revolution, then obtained an appointment at a French University where he remains to this day, teaching, as he put it, "French history to the French!"

My strongest supporter was an adult student by the name of Harvey Silvers, who was impressed by my "Hitler's Germany" course, which he took in the fall of 1975. A native of Chicago, Harvey was a self-made man, the first person in San Diego to manufacture hairpieces for individual clients. He got most of his customers at an annual fair in Del Mar. Now he was doing very well, with several employees. "All I need now is a little bit of culture," he said. "I'm getting there." A former socialist, he had become an active Zionist and defender of Israel. However, I found myself very much in sympathy with his distrust of Christianity. Behind the growing de-emphasis of the humanities in university curricula, for instance, he detected a religious Christianizing motive that did not want to raise problems and issues for discussion and analysis. Harvey did his best to keep me at SDSU, as noted in my journal on 27 February 1976:

"In teaching German history, he's gotta attack religion," he explained to Steffi. "There's no way he can teach the course without that. He can't do that in private colleges which draw their funds from religious groups." He supports me because I am "educating" San Diego college students. He is impelled by a genuine fear of repression, intolerance, and anti-Semitism in America. Beyond that he is impelled by a genuine revulsion against a mindless, unfeeling system in which educational values can be so distorted (e.g., in the administrative argument against continuation of temporary faculty members—"We need flexibility to serve student needs") and in which people can be treated so callously. He is impelled by a deep-seated feeling that rights must be constantly defended, abuses constantly challenged.

Although I didn't believe there was a real threat of a resurgence of classical antisemitism in the U.S. (and opposed the invocation of such a threat as an argument for Israeli expansion), I found myself encouraging Harvey's incipient paranoia, just to keep him so delightfully subversive! Harvey wrote a registered letter to the president of the university (who coincidentally became president of Kent State University a few years later, where Olaf headed the math department from 1976 on) to try to get him to change the rule against third-year temporary appointments. According to his report, Harvey also gave Neil Heyman a dressing-down for having volunteered to teach German history next year, appealing to his Jewish conscience! He even called up the German-American Club in San Diego to ask them if they had a job for me—as if to alert them to their duty to take care of their own!

In San Diego I also worked to extract some articles from my dissertation prior to revising it for publication as a book. A publication or two would certainly enhance my chances of getting a job, and completing a scholarly article looked more manageable and less time-consuming than converting my dissertation into a book, a more long-term project. The library resources at SDSU were limited, but the very good library at the University of California, San Diego, located in La Jolla an hour away, contained in its holdings the personal library of the famous historian Koppel Pinson (1904-1961). My article, "The Role of Heinrich von Stein in Nietzsche's Emergence as a Critic of Wagnerian Idealism and Cultural Nationalism," was published in the German journal *Nietzsche-Studien* in 1976. It allowed me to write the text in English while leaving all quotes in the original German—a great advantage in any publication dealing with Nietzsche! I had been attracted to Nietzsche since my undergraduate days when I discovered that he was one of the few non-Jewish German intellectuals of note who was not only entirely free of antisemitism, but also took an uncompromising stand against this malignant and growing politico-cultural movement at the end of the nineteenth century. To me his clarity on this particular question salvaged at least a remnant of German honor in the face of the more dominant rival aesthetic and political tradition, perhaps best personified by Richard Wagner, which defined Germany's exceptionalism in contradistinction to allegedly Jewish traits, such as materialism, commercialism, immoralism, and secularism. Nietzsche's response to the "Jewish question" still strikes me as exemplary today. "Let us rejoice in Jewish successes and achievements," he said (loosely paraphrased); "for they help us all." A Wagnerian in his youth, Nietzsche unequivocally repudiated German nationalism, ethnic supremacism, and political Romanticism in his later works. But Nietzsche was also sullied by his reputation as a power-monger whose vitalist philosophy had appealed to and was appropriated by many Nazi followers (though not by the more honest ones, who were quite aware that Nietzsche was their antagonist, not their ally). My liberal Harvard teacher Crane Brinton had written a devastating critique of Nietzsche during the war (as George Santayana [1863-1952]) had already done during the First World War). In college I could not yet claim to understand the full scope of Nietzsche's purpose in attacking Christianity and the Western moral tradition. My main effort in my oral examination on Nietzsche was to try to refute the conventional notion that Nietzsche was advocating or condoning ruthless competition in a perennial human contest for power and supremacy.

Nietzsche's purpose became much clearer to me once I understood what he was arguing against. That insight came as a result of my research into the Wagnerian and antisemitic intellectual tradition culminating in the openly racist publications of Houston Stewart Chamberlain (1855-1927), the Germanophile Englishman who embraced German nationalism with all the exaggerated fervor of a convert. An early and much less extreme exponent of Wagnerian *völkisch* nationalism was the talented but short-lived young aristocrat Heinrich von Stein (1857-1887), who had been engaged as the tutor of Wagner's children. Nietzsche saw in the thirteen-years-younger man an *alter ego* of his former self, before his bitter falling-out with Wagner in 1876. Hoping to enlighten Stein about the perils of Wagnerism and convert the promising youth to his own life-affirming philosophy, Nietzsche carried on a lively correspondence with Stein and invited him to a visit in Sils-Maria in 1884. Stein had just published a very conventional celebration of Germanic heroes and saints in the Wagnerian mode, to which Nietzsche responded cooly in December 1882: "As for 'the hero': I don't think as well of him as you do. Neverthelesss: it is the most acceptable form of human existence, especially if one has no other choice." One sentence in that same letter suddenly clarified for me what Nietzsche was trying to do: "*Ich möchte dem menschlichen Leben etwas von seinem herzbrecherischen und grausamen Charakter nehmen* (I would like to take from human existence some of its heartbreaking and cruel character)." No sooner have we come to love something, Nietzsche went on to explain, than the tyrant inside us, whom we like to call "our higher self," forces us to give it up. It was this nihilistic (i.e., life-denying) "ascetic ideal," so brilliantly dissected in *The Genealogy of Morals* (1886), that was the target of Nietzsche's ever more virulent attacks on Platonic idealism, world-renouncing Christianity, and the secular movements such as scientism, liberalism, socialism, and nationalism that rested on the same "nihilistic" metaphysical foundations. How different Nietzsche's conception of the self-overcoming *Übermensch* was from the battle-crazed warriors of Wagnerian myth! In my journal I noted that "one understands philosophers not by reading them, but by thinking about the problems they thought about."

This publication on one of the most important German philosophers in a peer-reviewed international journal no doubt helped to get me a temporary position at the University of Oregon for the 1976-1977 academic year. It was a replacement position for the well-known historian Roger Chickering, who had just received a Fulbright award to Germany. The offer from the University of Oregon came as a huge relief, very late in April 1976. I had already accustomed myself to the thought of unemployment, preparing to turn all my attention to supporting Steffi's business, which would probably become our main or even sole source of income. I even took lessons from a colleague of Steffi's in San Diego on how to cast silver jewelry, the "lost wax" method that

dependable) hatches an egg for a tropical bird. Because the elephant has promised to do this until the bird returns, he does not budge, even when derided by his fellow animals or captured by hunters for a circus. While the circus was playing Palm Beach, the bird—enjoying the easy life—happens to see the elephant. At the same time the egg finally hatches. Now the bird wants to reclaim it. But it turns out to be a flying elephant! The reward for perseverance! The elephant is America, the bird is decadent Western Europe. And Nazi Germany is repudiated by the triumph of environmentalism over the principle of heredity or race. What better repudiation of racialism than the transformation of a bird into an elephant simply because the elephant cared for the egg!

At the end of April 1975 the Vietnam adventure finally came to its ignominious close with the evacuation of the last American soldiers from the top of the American embassy building in Saigon (which was immediately renamed Ho Chi Minh City by the victorious communist forces). The following day I enjoyed one of the best and most successful classes I have ever taught. I opened up my introductory U.S. history class to students' reflections and comments on the dramatic events of the previous days. One after another student got up and, without any prompting, condemned the American intervention in the war and elaborated on what a huge mistake it had been. Having been careful not to introduce current politics into the classroom, I had no idea of the depth of opposition that these students harbored to the American role in the war. It was an educational moment that left me with enormous hope for and optimism about the future, even if dampened somewhat by the furious American bombardment of Cambodia in the wake of the seizure of the American merchant ship, the Mayaguez, on May 12th.

As was the case with most recent arrivals in San Diego, we had a succession of visitors anxious to experience the California lifestyle. Steffi's mother and her second husband Tümmi came in spring 1975. The old Nazi, then in his mid- to late sixties, admired the hang-gliders and surfers and said he wished he were young enough to engage in such dangerous sports as well. The following year it was Steffi's father's turn to visit. He came in January and February 1976, the best time of year to experience the dramatic difference between temperate and subtropical climates. Unfortunately all his photos were over-exposed. He had not counted on the intense light of the southern California sun. However, he was delighted to discover a pomegranate tree in our back yard. *"Das ist ja die reinste griechische Antike* (this is pure Grecian antiquity)!" he exclaimed. Gerhard, an architect by profession, also taught an adult education course in his hometown of Nuremberg on the psychological meaning of colors. He distinguished between two German words for "feeling," *Empfindung,* a corollary of the color red—the active quality of reacting to outside stimuli and hence able to forget—and *Gefühl,* the corollary of the color blue—the passive quality of internalizing outside stimuli and hence unable to forget. He was much given to performing psychological tests, one of which I recorded in my journal:

> He presented me with four squares on a page, each containing a dot, a line, or some other simple figure. His instructions were: "Draw something around them." I took this to mean that I was to enclose each figure in some way. My immediate temptation, for the sake of simplicity and because I felt I would be breaking the rule of spontaneity by thinking about more elaborate designs, was simply to draw a circle around each figure. The square with a dot seemed especially to invite such a simple solution. Then I thought that was too easy, and such an automatic response would reflect unfavorably on my personality, so—noticing a notation, *g. Selbstbewusstsein* (self-confidence) at the side of the sheet—I made a g out of the circle. Similarly I tried to add a twist to the circles I made around the other figures. These twists gravitated toward the bottom. Gerhard was marvelously shocked when he analyzed what I had drawn: *"Das ist ja ein Trauma! Du kommst von der Mutter nicht los* (you can't get away from your mother). There's something that is pulling you down to the *Mutterschoss* (mother's womb or lap). That is quite clear from all four drawings." Steffi was delighted. "I've always said that." Her exultation knew no bounds. But Gerhard was marvelously serious, as if there could be absolutely no doubt about the validity of his findings. *"Was ist es denn, das du nicht verarbeitet hast* (what is it you haven't worked through)? Maybe you can speak about it. That there is something from which you can't free yourself is quite clear."

My ultimate judgment on this experiment was rather spiteful:

In Gerhard one sees clearly the mental aberrations (astrology, color psychology, etc.) to which Germans, it seems, are driven by the lack of an appropriate mode for self-expression in the objective world.

Of course, I was very curious about Gerhard's take on Nazism, which he had experienced as a soldier in the non-commissioned ranks during the war. He did some very funny impersonations of strutting officers.

"*Mir ist alles Sektiererische verhasst* (I hate everything sectarian). That is what disturbed me about National Socialism."

When asked why he thought that Nazism had come to power in Germany, he gave three reasons:

First, the threat of Marxism. "I was not a proletarian and as a result I did not want to belong to the proletariat." Secondly, the need for unity. "There were so many national *Bünde* (associations) of all kinds, which supposedly were pursuing the same goal. One sensed that all that would have to be simplified, reduced to a lowest common denominator." Third, the Jewish problem. "We had six million unemployed, but no Jews were unemployed. They stuck together."

It was easy to see, however, that Gerhard must have had a hard time in the Nazi era. He was not a person who fit in easily anywhere, least of all in a highly regimented society.

For the summers of 1975 and 1976 we returned to Vermont, always varying our cross-country routes a bit and stopping for sight-seeing diversions on the way. Our stops on our return to San Diego in August 1975 included Syracuse, NY; Fremont, Ohio; Davenport, Iowa; York, Nebraska; Cheyenne, Wyoming; Evanston, Wyoming; St. George, Utah; and Victorville, California. Among the places we visited were Pioneer Village in Nebraska, Fort Bridger in Wyoming, the first state house in Fillmore, Utah, and several Spanish missions in California. Only an hour or so out of Irasburg, while still on Interstate 89, three-year-old Nicky asked, "Are those the Rocky Mountains?" On our museum stops Nicky had plenty of chance to use his newly-acquired expression "neato," a word he had picked up from Trina. In Iowa, angered that he was not allowed to buy candy at a roadside store, Nicky refused to return a pack of gum to the rack but instead threw it across the room. The shopkeeper reprimanded us: "You gotta lot of catchin' up to do. You can have your fun with him now, but he'll be a lot of trouble later." That prediction fortunately never came true. Nicky had some wonderful expressions when he wanted to be dressed or undressed in the morning or at night: "Put me on, Daddy," or "take me off, Daddy" (literal translations of the German *Zieh mich an* or *aus*). The climatic variations on our trip were quite stunning. In Nebraska it was too hot to have lunch outdoors, in Wyoming it was too cold to have breakfast outdoors. At a camp site in Green River, Wyoming, we were told by one of the natives, "You know what they call that stretch of road between Laramie and Cheyenne in winter? Ho Chi Minh trail." We marveled at some of the wonderful compound place names: Wagonhound Road, Sweetwater County, Medicine Bow, Big Blue Creek, Eight Mile Road. Dead Man's Wash, Horse Thief Basin. A sign in a barren Wyoming landscape read: "Keep Wyoming Green." Above it someone had painted in, "Smile." "Typical California small town," I noted in my travel journal as we were nearing our destination:

> The crests of "service organizations" (Lions, Rotary, Optimist, Kiwanis, Altrusia—with its slogan "patriotism, efficiency, service"—American Legion, Women's Professional League, etc.) prominently displayed at the entrance to the town, as if to warn against intruders who would disrupt the self-congratulatory homogeneity of the community.

Returning to Vermont in May 1976, we chose a southern route with stops in Gallup, New Mexico; Santa Rosa, New Mexico; El Reno, Oklahoma; Rolla, Missouri; Indianapolis; Youngstown, Ohio; and Poughkeepsie, New York. In the California desert we ran into a frightening sand storm that forced us to the side of the road for several hours. In my journal I noted:

> The Texas-sized pothole in the parking lot of a café in McLean, Texas, which caused the rear end to scrape bottom and sent the boxes in the back toppling forward. We feared it might have broken the rear axle— just the kind of accident which one so often has or hears of on trips of this kind. The leering, gloating faces of the bull-necked ranchers and cow-hands staring at us through the windows of the café.

The only damage, however, was to one of the gallon-size bottles of wine we were carrying in the back seat. It broke and left behind a wonderfully decadent aroma for most of the rest of the trip. Trina, who had been selected for a gifted class in San Diego (turning me from one day to the next from a critic to a champion of gifted education), learned the poem "The Distlefink" by heart to get free hamburgers at the Dutch Pantry restaurants en route.

The last show we had seen on public TV in San Diego was Somerset Maugham's "Quartet," prompting the following comment in my journal at the end of May 1976:

What makes him good is his commitment throughout the most insipid plots and stock characterizations and verbal diarrhea to the proposition (reappearing in one form or another in all his works) that "art is the only thing that matters, not wealth, not power, not love."

6

EUGENE, OREGON, 1976-1977

The insecurity of my employment status was beginning to take its toll on our marriage. Steffi was very reluctant to close up her shop again in Irasburg and trek back across the country for another temporary job with no realistic prospect of renewal. What's more, while in San Diego in September 1975 we had received the very disquieting news that someone had broken into our house in Irasburg and stolen some tools. Fortunately they did not get into the main part of the house, but only into the *Schuppen* (shed) in the back. Pretty much everyone in the village knew who the teen-aged burglar was, but nobody had any proof or was willing to provide it. From one day to the next, our home went from giving us a wonderful sense of security to posing a constant worry. In 1976 Steffi seriously considered staying in Irasburg all winter rather than relocating to another temporary location for another year and risking another episode of vandalism to our house. If she were to accompany me, she wanted to be persuaded to do so; I wanted it to be her own free decision—so that she would not complain later about *having* to be in Eugene and away from her beloved Vermont because of me. In the morning I felt strong enough to go it alone; in the evening I wanted the family to come along. Steffi felt the same way: in the morning she felt strong enough to cope by herself in Irasburg; in the evening she felt less inclined to go it alone, even in her beloved Irasburg home. We finally compromised: She and the children would join me in Eugene at the beginning of November and return to Vermont at the end of April. These were not particularly auspicious conditions for the long-term health of our relationship.

In late August I set off by myself for the Northwest in our VW bus, stopping off to visit my cousin Ellen (Edmonds) and her husband Roger Fleenor in Boise and spending a day with them at their vacation home in McCall.

Ellen and Roger Fleenor in Boise on my return trip, July 1977

In Eugene I rented a three-bedroom 1950s ranch-style house at 3425 Onyx Street and furnished it with rented furniture and things I picked up at the garage sales I scoured around town. Of all the temporary positions I held before finally settling in Spokane, the one at the University of Oregon was the most desirable one. This was not only because Eugene was a delightful place to be, with its youthful counter-culture still in full swing in the mid-1970s, but also because of the teaching conditions. Except for my graduate assistantships at the University of Massachusetts, this was my only experience of teaching at a "research university" in my entire career. After teaching four courses every semester at SDSU, three of them at the introductory level, I found the teaching load of two courses every semester at Oregon ideal for pursuing scholarly interests and projects. Of course, it did entail teaching graduate students in a PhD-granting department, which led to a certain peculiar conflict of interests, as in some cases I would actually find myself competing for jobs with the very students I was supposed to be training and promoting! But the additional challenge of teaching graduate students carried its own special rewards in intellectual stimulation and the opportunity to remain abreast of research trends at the cutting edges of the discipline. On the introductory level, my only (and very enjoyable) duty was to lecture to a large group of several hundred freshmen and sophomores twice a week on the history of western civilization in the modern era, while graduate teaching assistants conducted the small once-weekly discussion groups and handled all the grading. It is hard to overstate the relief that this liberation from the onerous responsibility of correcting exams and papers represented. It allowed me to put correspondingly greater effort into preparing my lectures and my upper-division courses, activities from which most university teachers derive their greatest pleasure and satisfaction. The obligation to do research that went along with the lightened teaching load felt much more like an opportunity than a chore.

In 1976 the second of the three articles I carved out of my dissertation appeared under the title, "Völkisch Literature: The Case of Friedrich Lienhard" in *The Wiener Library Bulletin*, a respected peer-reviewed journal on Jewish history and antisemitism published by the Institute of Contemporary Literature in London. Lienhard (1865-1929), an arch-conservative, Alsatian-born dramatist, novelist, and publicist, was one of the founders of the anti-urban, nativist *Heimatkunst* (local or regional art) movement in Germany at the turn of the century. By propagating *Heimatkunst*, Lienhard wanted to mobilize such traditional rural values as deference, duty, patriotism, and religious faith against the intellectual culture, permissive lifestyle, and social democracy of Berlin and other urban centers. Lienhard prided himself in his "idealism"—the rejection of "modern" materialistic values, among which he would have included the political values of liberalism, democracy, and socialism. The problem presented by such literary figures as Lienhard was how their "idealism" related to the militantly racist *völkisch* movement that emerged in strength in Germany in the late nineteenth century and culminated in Nazism after the First World War. "Respectable" conservatives like Lienhard criticized the "materialistic" racism and resort to violence of the radical right, but shared all their anti-democratic, anti-liberal, and anti-egalitarian values. While they rejected the violent tactics of the radical right, they could not help but embrace their general political perspective. This ambivalence, expressed in simplistic literary or journalistic forms, is what turned Lienhard's aesthetically undistinguished works into fascinating historical documents despite themselves. They unintentionally give readers insight into the mental and psychological contortions through which avowedly quiescent and "spiritual" conservatives rationalized the excesses of the radical right by attributing to them good, patriotic intentions even if their methods were flawed. Lienhard rejected racial justifications for his right-wing prejudices, but he did not reject the prejudices themselves; instead he gave them a "spiritual" justification, thus actually reinforcing and strengthening the very racism he ostensibly opposed. For me this insight from Lienhard's works became the key to the crucial question that all historians of Germany face at some point: how could the Nazis have gained power in a nation justly celebrated for its high culture, artistic creativity, and advanced level of civilization? The corollary question of course is, could it happen again? Many of these conservative "idealists" eventually turned against Nazism (especially *after* its defeat in the Second World War), but much too late, when the damage had already been done. For me there was an even larger lesson to be drawn from the often willing, sometimes grudging, but ultimately essential support that conservatives in Germany gave to Nazism: the importance of having national debates not just about political tactics or specific policies but about fundamental values, particularly the political values subsumed under the broad headings of "left" and "right." Lienhard's cautionary example also convinced me that at the heart of any truly liberal outlook is its rejection of the principle, "the ends justify the means." *Pacé* Lienhard, the means are always part of the ends, and political goals and the tactics needed to achieve them can never be neatly disjoined.

My reduced teaching load at the University of Oregon gave me the opportunity to complete the third of the articles I carved out of my dissertation. "Houston S. Chamberlain: From Monarchism to National Socialism" was published in *The Wiener Library Journal* in 1978. Chamberlain was quite a different kind of publicist than Lienhard. Like Lienhard, he had no artistic talent (nor, for that matter, any artistic pretensions), but he had scholarly pretensions, ideological ambitions, and a gift for language, which he used in writing his notorious two-volume, best-selling tract, *The Foundations of the Nineteenth Century* (1899-1900). This was an extraordinarily influential work that popularized a racialist interpretation of history. The purpose of

War-time passions allowed Chamberlain to openly spread a vision of German exceptionalism and world domination that he had expressed in his private correspondence with the monarch long before.

Chamberlain was also a devout fundamentalist Protestant, fearful not only of international Jewry but of international Catholicism as well. His example helped me to understand that religious faith was absolutely no guarantee against the perpetration of evil. Indeed, quite the opposite. Religious fundamentalism went hand-in-hand with hyper-nationalism in a way that we still see at the beginning of the twenty-first century. God and country merged as entities to be worshipped—as creative forces that could do no wrong. By blinding themselves to their own (self-)destructive impulses, fundamentalist "true believers" were the very source of the evil that they so readily projected onto non-believers and other outsiders. It was the Manichaean mentality itself—pitting "us versus them," "good versus evil," and epitomized in the notion "you're either with us or against us"—that was the cause of so much destruction in the world. When Chamberlain's *Foundations* first came out, one of Chamberlain's Wagnerian in-law relatives accused him of plagiarizing his ideas from the master without properly acknowledging his source. This was not quite fair, as Chamberlain did in fact repeatedly acknowledge his intellectual and political debt to the Wagnerian world view and to Wagner himself, about whom he had previously written several adulatory works. But it was a perceptive comment nonetheless. Chamberlain's work could be seen as Wagner's posthumous revenge against his apostate disciple, Nietzsche, whom Chamberlain roundly condemned for leaving the path of Wagnerian orthodoxy by preaching an anti-Christian and anti-nationalist world view "beyond good and evil." In my journal I wrote on 18 March 1977:

Nietzsche—stimulated to reflect upon "supermen" by Germany's imperial triumphs (and a conscience-ridden Lutheran upbringing). But the "slave revolt" that he condemns is the triumph of German philistinism. Not for a moment does he equate supermen with the makers of the new Reich, though the making of the new Reich may have made him think in the terms that he did. In a sense (overly dialectical, I suppose), Nietzsche is sympathizing with victims: the unsuspecting, unbegrudging, magnanimous, spontaneous, cheerful, open, (overly-)trusting, proud masters—the victims of the slave morality. It is not the masses as victims he despises, it is the masses as oppressors. Like Gobineau, Nietzsche was obsessed with the decline of aristocracy (he would have had to have been blind and deaf to have been indifferent to this nineteenth-century trend). But what a difference in the results of their respective reflections! Of course, Nietzsche *idealized* aristocracy even more than Gobineau. His idealism, absorbed in the very air he breathed, betrayed him into thinking material goods were inconsequential and demeaning.

When Steffi and the children joined me in Eugene via Canadian railway and Amtrak in November, 1975, we had already drifted apart to some degree, as manifested in a number of ways, including some most disconcerting episodes of sexual dysfunction on my part. No doubt contributing to my marital tensions was the rather close relationship I had developed with my congenial and attractive new colleague, Mavis Mate—the medievalist in the history department, who generously showed me the sights of the beautiful Willamette Valley.

With Mavis on an outing to Crater Lake, June 1977

Steffi was genuinely peeved at me for always being around in her dreams, thus preventing her from achieving fulfillment with the handsome young men who were vying for her attention in her dreams! Adding to our marital tensions was my very precarious employment status. At one point I drew hope when informed that the person I was replacing on the faculty, Roger Chickering, was considering extending his leave for another year. Chickering, who had trained under Gordon Craig at Stanford, was known to be unhappy about being relegated to a department not in the top ranks in terms of its national reputation. Although he did move to Georgetown University a few years later, Chickering turned down the opportunity to renew his Fulbright grant in 1977 and returned to Oregon for the 1977-1978 academic year, thereby forcing me to look for a position elsewhere. Other younger members of the Oregon faculty also went on to very distinguished careers at other universities. Foremost among these was Tom Brady, who went on to become one of the world's leading authorities on the German Reformation at Berkeley. A refreshingly radical and student-oriented voice at the sometimes rancorous meetings of an otherwise rather stodgy department, Tom was one of the leaders of the youthful, liberal faction in what was clearly a badly divided department. The corporate solidarity of the older faculty was not only based on their shared political conservatism, but also on their openly expressed disdain for student autonomy and what they perceived as an alarming decline in academic standards. Tom Brady and his wife, however, went out of their way to make us feel welcome in Eugene. Another colleague whom I only got to know briefly after his return from leave in April 1977 was Robert Berdahl, a nineteenth-century scholar a couple of years younger than me. Berdahl went on to a stunningly successful career as president of the University of Texas at Austin, then chancellor of the University of California system, and president of the Association of American Universities in 2006.

Inevitably, my best friends were two other temporary appointees in U.S. history who shared my (un)employment predicament. I particularly admired Eckard Toy, who had given up a tenured position at one of the subsidiary University of Wisconsin campuses several years earlier in solidarity with students who rallied for more open administrative policies and against what they felt was the university administration's complicity in the Vietnam War. Several years older than me, Eckard now found himself forced to seek temporary positions in an increasingly constricted job market. Although an Americanist, his research specialty—the American radical right—was topically related the radicals who thought they could use his class as a platform for radicalism. He deflated them by introducing historical information of which they were ignorant. Blankenship rubbed his hands at the thought: "You know, those guys who run at the mouth, who only know how things ought to be, but have no conception of where we've been or where we're at right now."

Eckard, Warren, and I got along very well indeed, despite the almost unavoidable rivalry imposed on us by our temporary status, leading Steffi to comment, "*Ihr könnt gar nicht Freunde sein* (there's no way you can be friends)". The following entry in my journal on 16 March 1977 seemed to prove her right:

I must guard against bitterness and I must guard against paranoia. The latest instance of the latter: learning from Eckard that Warren Blankenship had applied to Reed College for the same position as I had and may have stayed over after a conference in Portland to try to get an interview. Feeling of being betrayed, not because he doesn't have as much right to the position as I do, but because his failure to tell me seems to prove that he sets no great store by our friendship. Also, anger at his initiative—he called them—and the feeling that it is unfair that he should get the job not on his merits alone, but because he went after it. And then the reflection—strangely something of a comfort—that the system bred competition and conflict among those at the bottom, and it did so in order to prevent solidarity. It did so to the benefit of those who hogged the lions' share of benefits that the system can confer.

This led to a further reflection:

Conventional wisdom has it that communism flourishes in times of economic scarcity. Logically it should be so. One would expect the dispossessed to band together. But in actual fact it may be that fascism benefits most by conditions which create a proletariat (the unemployed) *below* the working class, thus making the latter anxious to maintain their status as job-holders against those below.

125

To be fair, however, most of the University of Oregon history department, at least the younger ones we associated with, sympathized with our plight. Jack Maddex, a historian of the American South, called us exploited "migrant labor" and Joe Esherick, an Asia specialist, appreciatively referred to us as "itinerant preachers."

Despite the hope engendered by Jimmy Carter's victory in the presidential election in November 1976, it was becoming clear that the conservative tide that would overwhelm the country a few years later was growing, and the progressive changes in popular consciousness resulting from the 1960s movements were not only petering out, but going into reverse. The economy of the mid- to late 1970s bred a new word in the American vocabulary, "stagflation"—the unexpected combination of inflation and unemployment. The conservative, nationalistic, anti-liberal movement started by Goldwater in 1964 to dismantle the "welfare state" and devote more resources to fighting communism did its best to exploit the popular anger and disaffection generated by economic decline. Ronald Reagan, who had already unsuccessfully challenged the nominally more liberal Gerald Ford for the Republican nomination in 1976, led the growing backlash against not only the 1960s, but against Roosevelt's New Deal and Johnson's Great Society as well. When he came to Eugene in June 1977, he also criticized the Carter Administration's ongoing Strategic Arms Limitation Treaty (SALT) talks with the Soviet Union, calling for the U. S. to play its trump card, "which is to say, 'Okay, we're going to turn our industrial machine into developing weapons'…and the Soviet Union knows there's no way in the world they could keep up with us."

Even I found myself somewhat ambivalent about affirmative action programs that were coming under increasing attack from the right, but were also a potential hindrance to me in applications to departments actively recruiting women candidates. The widely publicized Marco De Funis case, a suit won by a rejected applicant against the University of Washington Law School for reverse discrimination, because several Black applicants with inferior academic records and test scores had been admitted, drew the following comment from me in February 1977:

[Like De Funis] I would have been bitter, but I would not have fought it. That's the difference. Fighting is necessary: to *lose* bitterness!

At the University of Oregon I was unexpectedly reunited with my old college friend Gordon Goles (1934-2007), by now a prominent scientist in the geology department, widely recognized for his pioneering work on the chemical composition of stones retrieved from the moon. He took the initiative to contact me, a gesture for which I was very grateful, as I'm not at all sure whether I would have had enough gumption to overcome my embarrassment about my lowly professional status to contact him. We met again for the first time since our college years at a Bach chamber music concert at which good old Gordon, very much in character, jumped to his feet to lead the enthusiastic applause. Unfortunately, our communications lapsed again after I left Oregon in July 1977. I had hoped to see him again at our fiftieth Harvard reunion in 2006, but he was not in attendance. Perhaps he was as averse to class reunions as were both of my roommates, Paul Russell (before his premature death in 1996) and Sy Goldstaub.

My job insecurity and marital tensions affected my health in Eugene. I was diagnosed with ulcerative colitis, after a colonoscopy, which in those days was still done without any anaesthetic. Some years later, after a more thorough examination (with anaesthesia), my diagnosis was changed to the much milder though still chronic condition labeled "lymphocytic colitis." At one point my weight dropped to 135 pounds. Steffi rather predictably blamed my malady on Mama, at least by implication. On 25 November 1976 she commented on my upset stomach after Thanksgiving dinner: "*Du kannst nicht kotzen, weil du dich vor nichts ekelst. Das ist weil du im Schmutz aufgewachsen bist* (you can't vomit because nothing disgusts you. That's because you grew up in dirt)." But she sympathized with me: "*Du hast es schwer gehabt. Mama hasst alles Schwache* (you had a hard time. Mama hates everything weak)." Indeed, it was that summer that Mama explained her new-found admiration for Aleksandr Solzhenitsyn (1918-2008), who had settled in Vermont, by asserting, "I like people who are absolutely sure of themselves." What she disliked in people, she explained, was the "worm's-eye view." The conflict between my mother and my wife made me wonder whether the only way I could "cut the umbilical cord" was to cut my marriage ties as well. Steffi also felt vindicated by the description of colitis in our *Gesundheitsbuch* (a health manual for the home): "*Eine Krankheit, die sich mit Vorliebe verkrampfte Gemüter aussucht* (a disease that seeks out tense and rigid temperaments)." I took some satisfaction from the fact that colitis was an auto-immune disease.

I was allergic to myself, which rather accurately described how I often felt! I was also officially diagnosed with lactose intolerance, although it was clear to me that I had been suffering from this condition ever since the war.

In Eugene, beside Steffi's workbench, 1977

Colitis forced me to adopt a healthier lifestyle. For a full year I entirely gave up alcohol, not only alleviating my symptoms but also occasionally making me feel quite smug about my self-discipline. Here is how I described my reaction to a faculty party on 14 May 1977:

Ten minutes into Karen's [Achberger] party for Mavis yesterday, the sobering question occurred to me: "What am I doing here? Whatever impelled me to come?" Normally I then would have proceeded to get drunk. Compelled by my colitis to remain sober, I came away from the party feeling extremely good about my disciplined conduct. But I regretted my lack of courage in having risen only to the level of conventional party chatter.

In December 1976 we visited our Vermont "hippie" friends, Paul and Sandy Raynor, who had moved (only temporarily, as it turned out) to the Oregon coast—attracted by the state's mild climate, scenic beauty, and ecological consciousness in their futile search for the ideal counter-cultural community. Paul, of mixed Korean-American parentage, was a painter, quite devoted to his art, but also determined to lead a self-sufficient rural life free of commercial constraints. His quest for authenticity had impressed me years before when he told me, "I don't want to find myself at the age of forty stuck in a job I don't like." In Vermont he had built three log-houses in succession for his family, each one larger and sturdier than the one before, but he was forced to abandon the last one, a building of truly palatial dimensions, when the bank financing he had uncharacteristically applied for ran out. We acquired quite a few of Paul's provocatively gothic paintings, some of which we paid for in cash and others we traded for with Steffi's jewelry. Sandy had grown up in the same northwest corner of Connecticut as we Stackelbergs, and though younger than us, she had heard all about us from our mutual friends, the Kügelgens. On the beach only a few hundred yards from the cottage Paul and Sandy had rented on the Oregon coast we dug up the huge clams peculiar to that area. Paul and Sandy tried to help us resolve the marital tensions that they had noticed and we did not try to conceal. They suggested that a temporary sexual partner swap might serve a therapeutic purpose, but neither Steffi nor I were interested. We reacted in different ways, however; Steffi cried at the prospect of the end of our marriage that Paul and Sandy's proposition implied, while I went into an equally uncontrollable laughing fit at the preposterous nature of their proposed therapy! It was clear that Paul had hoped to sleep with Steffi. My revenge was to decline the opportunity to sleep with Sandy! Perhaps inevitably, Paul and Sandy's open marriage dissolved even sooner than ours, leaving Sandy to raise three daughters on her own.

Although I had never formally studied the Hegelian dialectic, it seemed to me as if life was almost daily teaching me what it meant in practice. The ever-present threat of unemployment also cleared my mind for egalitarian ideas that questioned the inequitable *status quo*. It was part of a continuing radicalization process that ultimately made me ready to openly acknowledge my preference for a socialist transformation of society and to do what I could to realize that goal—from within the social institutions in which I was compelled to operate if I wished to support my family and exercise any influence at all. I have subsequently been accused of hypocrisy for advocating socialist change while living a bourgeois lifestyle. Even my son Nick once asked me why I didn't move to Russia if I liked communism so much. I retorted that I wouldn't want to give the Right that satisfaction: right-wingers would be delighted for socialists to give away all their property including the shirts off their backs! How better to disable any opposition to corporate domination and control? In my journal I left a superficial, unsystematic, and incomplete record of some of the examples of the dialectical nature of life and thought that I began to see everywhere, especially in the politics of the continuing Cold War:

12 Apr 1976 The dialectic: one can care very greatly about radical social reform, but dislike equally greatly the individual exponent of such reform.

5 Jul The greatest defense for the study of history: all misunderstandings occur because ideas (or events) are apprehended in isolation rather than in their social context. That is also the weakness of non-dialectical, linear thinking.

21 Jul Nietzsche and Marx: saint and sinner? The trouble with Marx is that he slept with his housekeeper, the trouble with Nietzsche is that he didn't (not that we know of, anyway)! Nietzsche's thought too much a product of his life; Marx's life not enough a product of his thought.

The true Golden Mean will even balance moderation—with occasional excess! Moderation must be *tempered* by excess.

19 Sep Equality leads to progress because it evens out competition: it puts people on the same level, in the same arena. It equalizes the conditions of competition. It levels the playing field. It eliminates the artificial barriers to true competition: the barriers created by wealth, position, hierarchical structures, habits of deference. In education this

is clearly visible. Professors are challenged today as never before. They can no longer pontificate *ex cathedra*.

16 Nov How to explain the dialectic? Where are the best examples? Perhaps in the changing meaning of words? "Appeasement" used as a positive term ("reconciliation") at Locarno. "Pacification" and its changed meaning in Vietnam.

The dialectic of Marx, who set out to help mankind with a doctrine that inflicted suffering and woe, and Nietzsche, who had no similar humanitarian impulse, yet whose philosophy has a therapeutic effect on individuals.

12 Dec Was this Barry Marks's [one of my students at SDSU] point on the thinking process falling into dialectical patterns without fail? You cannot think out a pure truth outside the realm of vulgar positivist fact (the barn is red). You always run into contradictions. Two perfectly valid truths may be diametrically opposed to each other (e.g., the desirability of both liberty and equality). The dialectical nature of life (truth in totality) is what makes debate so difficult. It is what makes it possible to accuse egalitarians of elitism—because they actively advocate egalitarianism, i.e., they want to get people to accept it, hence they proceed from an elitist assumption: I know best what is good for you (or us).

Further example: liberalism is emancipating—but precisely because it frees individuals from restraint, it gives rise to resentments and competitive rivalries, which in turn lead to a longing for the re-imposition of restraint upon one's rivals. Liberalism gives rise to its own antithesis. The contradictions are even more intrinsic than the foregoing would suggest: liberalism itself makes it possible—by granting the requisite freedom—for some to restrain (or exploit) others. The contradiction is built in. By the same token you cannot achieve total equality because of the absence of total uniformity. Every breath upsets the balance. The horror in the present confrontation between socialism and liberalism is not that they are at odds, but that both—unwittingly in league in this respect—are giving birth to what will destroy them both:

militarism, global war. The dialectic is insidious, not obvious; complex, not simple. A variety of contradictions are constantly intersecting. And often contradictions do not emerge as such until the war between them is already on (or over!) We do not recognize that our defenders of liberalism are undermining it.

The dialectic of psychology and sociology, of psychological motivation and sociological causation. (It takes a certain kind of person to be a Marxist.) This is what makes psychohistory so difficult, so problematical.

The dialectic in day-to-day situations: [Gustav] Alef [an older conservative faculty member] wants to convince me of the low standards in the department. "Is this a distinguished department?" he asks. I answer "yes" in order not to second his argument, but in secret I agree with him: what makes the department undistinguished is that people like Alef are in it, riding their sinecures!

16 Jan 1977 One implication of the dialectic is that you *cannot* think out solutions to problems. By trying to do so you get hopelessly lost down one-way alleys. What you come up with will even make some sense. But other one-way alleys pointing in other directions will make equal sense. Truth (always provisional, never absolute) only emerges in practice. Thought must be brought to bear to recognize it. But thought alone is useless, even pernicious, because misleading.

21 Jan One can favor both liberty and equality, as liberals do, but one must realize that without equality there can only be liberty for some, not all.

31 Jan A world of general equality provides better hope for personal liberty than a world of liberty does for equality. A world divided provides neither.

11 Feb Liberals learn to live with "pluralism," but they don't learn to live with the "dialectic."

20 Feb Situation today not unlike the *Ancien Regime* of the late eighteenth century: PhD's (like titles of nobility) easy to acquire (for sale!), but ladders of hierarchy harder to climb.

24 Feb Why it is important to keep alive the consciousness of the anti-Marxist, anti-humanitarian, anti-egalitarian thrust of fascism: fighting fascism is what makes us realize our collective responsibility, our responsibility for our fellow humans.

12 Mar Perhaps the fatal divergence in western civilization *did* come with the rise of modern science—not because it has turned us to materialism and exhausted our resources, and upset our ecology, but because it made us ask "how" of things rather than "why." Not because it introduced skepticism and criticism, but because it eliminated a truly critical attitude. Proposal: call the humanities and social sciences the "critical sciences."

14 Mar American society institutionalizes competition; Soviet society institutionalizes cooperation. The former produces hardship, the latter strait-jacketing.

18 Mar The principle of compensatory nature (Emerson) and the principle of the dialectic are of course one and the same. But the former is an expression of Nietzschean *amor fati*, the latter of Marxian revolutionary activism—the will to change the world.

26 Mar The liberal fallacy: to worry only about the loss of freedom (imprisonment of dissidents in the USSR) rather than the loss of livelihood or prosperity. Callousness about unemployment. Insensitivity to the hardships—psychological and physical—of unemployment and underemployment. A "prosperity" based only on GNP and not on the general welfare is fraudulent. Liberals worry about being thrown into prison (or mental hospitals) because of their ideas—usually ideas that are useful in maintaining the prerogatives of those who benefit from a liberal system. But they care much less about people who are thrown into hospitals (or prisons) for lack of money. Beware the hypocrisy! It is as dangerous as an H-bomb! They talk about freedom of ideas, but not

about the middle-class comforts which economic freedom protects at the expense of the less fortunate. The excluded in a socialist state (liberal dissidents) are a far smaller minority than the excluded in a liberal state (the impoverished). The victims of socialism—those who refuse to go along with the communitarian ethos—must be put in jail for the system to function effectively. The victims of economic liberalism—the impoverished—can be safely left to fend for themselves as long as they remain deferential and at least tacitly accept the individualist ethos. Their poverty will render them ineffectual in any case. Socialism creates more opportunities for (or categories of) crime because more forms of exploitation or anti-social behavior are stigmatized than under liberalism (capitalism).

30 May Mama's "You can't fool those below": Those above are easily blinded by their vested interest in the *status quo*. How can they be expected to perceive the dialectical nature of historical change—except as a terrible threat? Above all the legitimacy of dialectical change must be questioned. Nothing could be more threatening than to regard such change as inevitable.

12 Jun The disgust engendered by Eldridge Cleaver, the reborn Christian. A turncoat, a betrayer of revolution. But maybe not. Maybe his career is just another example of the cunning of reason: no longer analyzing Babylon's decadence, he contributes to it—unwittingly. Perhaps he digs its grave more effectively than he could have as a revolutionary ...Or is this only wishful thinking?

It was not until May, after Steffi and the children had already returned to Vermont, that my employment dilemma was resolved, at least for the following academic year. I received an invitation for a campus interview at the University of South Dakota for a one-year appointment to replace their German history specialist, Donald Pryce, who had received a research fellowship at one of the California universities. My visit went surprisingly well, despite a bout of the colitis that had plagued me all year. But in another example of the law of compensation in nature, my illness had a relaxing effect, putting all my other troubles into soothing perspective. I gave a strong and confident presentation and unexpectedly got the job.

7

VERMILLION, SOUTH DAKOTA, 1977-1978

In a way, the replacement position at the University of South Dakota was another step back. My salary was $12,000 for the year, $2,000 less than my starting salary at San Diego State University three years earlier. But I was absolutely delighted to get the job, and as long as we lived frugally, as we did, we could get by on my earnings and the income from Steffi's jewelry. We soon discovered the advantages of the business-friendly American system of taxation with its generous deductions for business-related expenses. The loopholes and tax credits designed to serve the interests of large corporations are indefensible. But the basic system allowing small businesses to deduct actual living expenses such as heating costs, phone bills, and other upkeep is quite essential to the financial well-being of self-employed crafts persons, especially when they work out of their own homes.

As in the previous year in Eugene, I proceeded ahead and Steffi followed with Nicky at the end of October. But this time Trina accompanied me to Vermillion, as she was now entering sixth grade and we thought it best that she start the school year at her new school—her fourth school in six years. Nicky started first grade in Irasburg and then continued at the same grade level in Vermillion, a decision we later regretted as it put him a year ahead of himself for the rest of his school career. He made the varsity baseball team as a high school senior in Spokane, but graduated at seventeen before he had reached his full height and strength. Trina and I set out for South Dakota on 21 August, 1977, reaching the Chicago area on August 24th and our destination the following day. En route I experienced the following epiphany, playing cards with my bright eleven-year-old daughter:

Defeated at the game of "Liar" by Trina despite my best efforts. Feeling more and more aggravated not just by Trina's success in fooling me (the idea is to get rid of one's cards by hook or crook, but if one is caught, one must take the whole pile), but by her manner of absorbing setbacks without psychological defeat: a continuous laughter not apparently warranted by events, but most disconcerting to opponents already baffled by her strategy. For the brief time of the game I could sympathize strongly with Nicky, who is of course always in the position I found myself in, unwillingly, in this game.

We made occasional sightseeing stops along the way, one of them at Herbert Hoover's birthplace in West Branch, Iowa:

Defensive tone throughout, trying to exonerate Hoover from culpability in the depression. Isolated quotes from obscure speeches framed and spot-lighted to show that he was *not* unfriendly to labor interests. He even called on private insurance companies to go into unemployment insurance in the 1920s! A newspaper column from 1935 (!) assured the visitor that Hoover had tried to warn against over-speculation in the late twenties. Much coverage of Hoover's war relief work, but no mention of "Hoovervilles" or the Bonus Army. But, surprisingly, his negative reputation may have produced a positive effect. The building is much less ostentatious than the Truman, Eisenhower, Kennedy, or Johnson libraries. There wasn't much there, and less is better in these things. The attendants, too, seemed friendlier, more personable, as if grateful that we should have bothered to stop by.

Vermillion was a picturesque little town, close to the Missouri River. It looked more like a farming village than a university town, except that it had more bookstores than one would have expected to find on the prairie. I actually experienced a greater culture shock on first coming to Vermillion than either in San Diego or Eugene, where the differences from the East Coast were less noticeable. A feeling of isolation was hard to avoid. The closest town of any size was Sioux City across the border in Iowa, about twenty miles away. Sioux Falls, the home of South Dakota State University and today also of a branch campus of the University of South Dakota, was sixty miles to the north. We soon discovered that for permanent residents the destination of choice for relief from rural monotony and cultural aridity was Minneapolis, some 200 miles to the northeast. We settled into the comfortable Craftsman-style home at 116 North Yale Street of Donald Pryce, the faculty member I was replacing for the year. The department faculty, fewer than a dozen, was a close-knit group with quite a bit of friendly socializing among them. We were immediately included in their various activities, including tennis, and, in bad weather, basketball. I was somewhat disconcerted, however, by their shared disdain for their hometown, out "in the middle of nowhere." When the first winter storm struck in early October, I experienced some of the disadvantages of the harsh continental climate to which they were subject. But as someone desperately trying to get a foothold in the profession, being stuck in a place like the University of South Dakota did not seem like the worst fate to me! This was not the dominant consensus among my colleagues, however. Most of them actually envied me for *not* having tenure, because it meant that I didn't face the prospect of having to spend a good part of my life out in the sticks. I was free (in the sense of being unhindered by inner restraints, such as prudence) to look for another job. In my journal I noted that in their view "the very fact that I *have to* look for a job provides me with the same kind of advantage as a binding deadline does for someone who needs to get a project done." The younger members of the department were frequently applying for positions elsewhere, usually deanships in the hopes that the administrative path might provide a means to get away. They were also very aware that only through publications could they hope to improve their career chances. Teaching, no matter how conscientious, was not going to get the job done. As the chair of the department, Steve Ward, blithely put it, "We teach for show and write for dough."

I shared an office with young Bob Hilderbrand, a tall, athletic, easygoing native of neighboring Iowa and a University of Iowa PhD who was replacing an American historian on sabbatical for the year. He eventually managed to gain a permanent position at USD, where, unlike most of his colleagues, he felt quite at home—so much so, in fact, that in 1977 he contemplated staying in Vermillion the following year even if his job was not renewed. In the event, however, he went on to spend his entire career at USD. Bob represented the best of "prairie populism," an open-minded, progressive attitude worthy of the state's popular senior senator, George McGovern. Bob was flush with the confidence of youth.

"I know I will write novels some day," he told me. "I've got it in me. It's just a question of when it will come out. Writing novels for me is a diversion. I can do it in my free time." Whether he ever wrote those novels I don't know, but he did write several excellent history monographs, including what is probably the leading academic study of the Bretton Woods Monetary Conference after the war and the origins of the United Nations. He was not a pedant, but he did take his responsibility for teaching the correct rules of grammar to his students very seriously. "Now at the start of my career I have to make a fundamental decision," he said. "Am I going to enforce the correct usage of the pronouns 'which' and 'that,' or is insisting on this distinction just a hopeless cause?" Bob and his wife were Mormons, which led to an amusing misunderstanding at one of our social gatherings. As cream and sugar were circulating after dinner in anticipation of the coffee to come, we both made reference to the approaching poison. "No such decadence!" we agreed. But whereas I meant the cream (because of my lactose intolerance), he meant the coffee!

I soon became aware of the peculiar sartorial obsessions of the department, which always made me feel somewhat negligent in my personal appearance. Perhaps it was the informality of life on the prairie that made the university-connected personnel so conscious of dress and so enamored of formal attire. Our chairman Steve Ward, a historian of Britain, set the tone. His improbable model was the sophisticated British don. It struck me as ironic that in the heart of the Great Prairies, of all places, I should encounter the greatest sensitivity to proper dress. Bob Hilderbrand rationalized his habit of wearing ties every day as a way of distinguishing himself from his students. "Otherwise I'd be completely one of them," he said. This led me to reflect that I deliberately avoided wearing ties—in order to reduce the distance between myself and my students. "My accent is what skin color is to Blacks," I wrote in my journal. "Try as I may, I can't blend in. It is an involuntary badge of otherness." Bob's easy relations with his students and other members of the department made me even more conscious of my involuntary outsider status. In the spring of 1978 I reflected on the department's sartorial conventions:

> The tennis game last fall as Ward's partner against Wolff and Watterson: only now do I realize what a *faux pas* it was to have taken off my jersey. Only now do their rules and conventions exert their constraints on me. Only now do I realize that my failure to wear tie and coat to classes—

more a token of conformity than of rebellion on my part—must strike them as perverse. This is especially noticeable when one of them doesn't wear tie or coat: it appears not just out of place but out of character. One feels sorry for and slightly contemptuous of him. His democratic or liberal gesture just seems like backsliding.

Nonetheless my reaction to South Dakota was overwhelmingly positive:

So much easier to get a handle on it than on California (or just San Diego) or Oregon. In fact it seems as if California and Oregon only now fall into place in the light of my experience of South Dakota. I *should* feel less comfortable here, but I don't. Perhaps it is because I am basically a missionary type—and here I really do have a mission: teaching the critical approach to students who study history for its conservative, antiquarian appeal, and, even more difficult, teaching critical German history to students of largely German stock who want to hear what's good about their country of origin and their past.

With Hilderbrand I attended the AHA annual meeting in Dallas in December 1977 in search of a job for the following year. I placed some hopes in an interview I had scheduled with the representative of Hampshire College, Anson Rabinbach. He was the well-known editor of the outstanding journal *New German Critique* and today is a professor at Princeton University. However, he cancelled the interview at the last moment, pleading too much to do and leaving the dozens of candidates who had signed up angry and disappointed. Some of us even went so far as to write a letter of complaint to the AHA, pointing out that such late cancellations not only meant the loss of that particular interview but of a valuable time slot, as it was then too late to sign up for an alternate interview. No wonder the job fairs at annual meetings came to be referred to sarcastically as "meat markets." The incident led me to reflect on the apparently unavoidable dialectic of the personal and the political in movements of the left:

The "callousness" of the party functionary in a cause ultimately designed to rid the world of callous relations; but you can't be "humane" to every individual and effectively further the cause.

I helped my own cause that spring by becoming the only USD faculty member to give a paper at the annual Mid-American History Conference in Omaha, Nebraska, for which I had applied as soon as I learned that I would be teaching in South Dakota that year. The paper was a spin-off of my work on H. S. Chamberlain's World War I pamphlets and precipitated an animated discussion. My session moderator, Evelyn Haller, paid me a compliment, "That was the liveliest session I've ever been at," and wished me well in my job search: "You have so much to offer." Steve Ward also appreciated my initiative, an appreciation reflected in the excellent recommendations he wrote for my job applications that spring. The job hunt continued to absorb much of my time, inducing me to write in my journal of "my fear that by refusing to permit myself to hope for success in the job hunt (in order to avoid disappointment) I am actually failing to mobilize all potential resources in that hunt." My most promising opportunity once again came late in the year. In the first week of May 1978 (the last week of classes) I was invited to a campus interview at Gonzaga University in Spokane. A Jesuit university was the last place I expected to end up, but the interview went surprisingly well. The topics of the trial class I was asked to teach were fascism and Nazism, the subjects closest to my research interests and field of specialization. I was fortunate, too, in that it was an honors class in Western Civilization that I was given to conduct. It was not hard to get its bright students to ask questions and participate in the discussion. At the end I got an additional boost when on leaving the classroom several students urged the assembled departmental faculty to "hire him" and "sign him up."

A few days later I received a call from the departmental chair, Father Tony Via, informing me that the department had voted unanimously to offer me the position. I was so thrilled by this offer that I accepted it on the spot. Fr. Via urged me to take the full forty-eight hours they were willing to grant me before making so important a commitment, but I didn't want to take the risk that by some unlucky fluke their offer might yet be withdrawn! In retrospect I realized that my eagerness might have come across as desperation, a reaction that was not likely to enhance the value they might attach to their new acquisition. It might have been more politic to leave them with the impression that in hiring me they had beaten out strong competition for my services from other prestigious universities! This was not the case, however. It was I who had beaten out what I later learned were 125 applicants for the job (only one of whom, however, besides me, was invited to campus for an interview). I did receive two additional tenure-track offers in the days that followed (my first tenure-track offers since getting my PhD in 1974), but they were not of a kind to make me regret having made too hasty a decision in choosing Gonzaga. One was from Kansas Wesleyan, where I would have constituted the entire history department with responsibility for all fields from ancient to modern. The only thing going for Kansas Wesleyan was my admiration for the Methodists for having opposed the British slave trade so fiercely in the nineteenth century. The other tenure-track offer was from Fayetteville State College in North Carolina, an all-African-American college with a teaching load of five courses per semester. Accepting this arduous assignment might have eased my conscience about failing to fulfill the community service obligations of my Leadership Development Fellowship back in 1970, but I can't say that I regretted my commitment to Gonzaga even for a moment.

Painting Easter eggs in Vermillion, SD, spring 1978

That spring I read that Bob Hope would be the commencement speaker at Gonzaga this year. His invitation seemed a fitting way to commemorate the untimely death of his friend and Gonzaga's most illustrious alumnus, Bing Crosby, of a heart attack on a golf course in Spain a few weeks earlier. Crosby, a native of Spokane, never actually graduated from Gonzaga, having left for Hollywood with his band as an undergraduate before receiving his degree, but he became one of the university's most generous donors. In the 1950s he had provided the funding for Gonzaga's library, and during my recruiting visit there was some speculation that he might have left some of his sizable estate to his *alma mater*. This was not the case, however, as he had turned against the university in the 1970s when the anti-war movement began making inroads among students and faculty even in such hotbeds of conformity and conservatism as Spokane. Gonzaga was certainly not untouched by the emancipating trends of the late 1960s and 1970s. While on my recruiting visit I had the chance to read the President's Report, which featured an essay by the university president, Fr. Bernard Coughlin, on the importance of addressing the problem of social and economic inequality. The Jesuit order had only recently announced its celebrated "option for the poor," giving top priority to its mission of social justice. The Jesuits were particularly active in missions in Central America, where social conflict was rife and liberation theology was beginning to take root, especially among the base communities of the un-propertied and dispossessed. I was surprised and cheered when Fr. Via compared the present moment in time to the Church's belated but ultimately successful efforts to come to terms with secular liberalism and capitalism in the nineteenth century: "It's time that we came to terms with the socialist movement as well." There was even some talk of making peace, not with the Soviet system, to be sure, but with Euro-Communism, which was then enjoying its brief ascendancy in Italy. When the tide again turned after Reagan's election in 1980, I found myself in an unexpectedly contentious struggle for tenure against the conservatives in the department. I thanked my lucky stars that I had been hired at a time when the Jesuits were still so open to egalitarian values and causes.

Steffi and the children were already back in Vermont when I told her of my new job over the phone. Her reaction was unexpected: "*Vielleicht werden wir noch fromm* (maybe we'll yet become pious)!" My USD colleagues were very happy for me. I could tell that my stature had risen in their eyes when Steve Ward—always impressed by outward appearances—said, "I didn't know you had such a new VW van!"

8

AT HOME IN SPOKANE? 1978-1980

In early August I set out with our loaded van for Spokane—this time, for a change, via Canada and northern Michigan, connecting with Interstate 94 in Minneapolis. Having accumulated enough savings for a small down payment, we had rather optimistically decided to buy a house in Spokane in the hope that this would be our final station in my seemingly endless search for a permanent teaching job. I planned to drive to Spokane with some of our belongings, buy a house, and fly back east before returning with Trina to Spokane for the start of the semester in early September. As usual, I kept a bit of a travel diary, beginning with an entry in North Bay, Ontario, on August 9, 1978:

> Snack bar in Whiteriver, Ontario. Ordering a "butter tart," but sending it back when I saw it had a rich dairy-based filling. "You mean you didn't know what a butter tart was? They been out a long time." But then the waitress-owner relented. "It's not so unusual, eh? When I first got married I didn't know what celery was. I grew up around Niagara Falls, we never grew it, and we couldn't afford to buy such stuff. When I saw my husband eat it I thought it was some sort of green pepper."

The next day in Ishpenning, Michigan, I noted "the smokestacks amid the forests on the banks of Lake Superior" and "the reverse side of the coin: railways still 'disfigure' Canadian villages." I was subjected to an

Attack of mosquitoes at a rest area in Jacobson, Minnesota, forcing and
following me into the car. Turning on the radio, I am informed: "That
mosquito bite might be more serious than you thought. Investigations
are still under way into whether the death of an eight-year-old Windham
boy was caused by encephalitis borne by mosquitoes."

The radio was my constant companion, offering me such apothegms as
Malcolm Muggeridge expounding on the uniqueness of the Jews: "God is
their king. There are no Caesars." I spent the night of August 11th in Fargo,
North Dakota, noting that the entire town smelled "like my breakfast bran
buds." It must have been a seasonal thing, because on our return trip the
following spring, the smell was entirely absent. In Miles City, Montana, I was
impressed by the ubiquity of the wide-brimmed Western hats. I recorded a

Dream of having an insight about Mama and recording it in my journal,
to wit that she had experience of only two countries, the U. S. and
Germany, and that this experience was alike. Both countries "always
wanted more."

My final stop before Spokane was in Bearmouth, Montana, thirty-five miles
east of Missoula—the first destination I did not make on schedule. In Spokane
the next day I was heartened by a sign in front of a church: "Failure is the
path of least persistence."

I stayed at the Shamrock Motel on Sprague Avenue, the main East-West
business street, while searching for an affordable house with the prearranged
help of a local real estate agent. She was quite enthusiastic at first, but her
interest declined rather noticeably when she found out that my starting salary
at Gonzaga would be only $14,000. I soon discovered that houses in the most
attractive residential area, the South Hill, were priced beyond our means. The
next best option, it seemed, was to buy a house in the Mission district, within
walking distance of the Gonzaga campus. I made an offer on a $32,000 house
on Augusta Avenue, which was in fact accepted. However, only a half-hour
later, my agent called me at my motel, informing me that the owners had
changed their minds. Apparently I had made the mistake, while touring the
house, of telling my agent rather too loudly what a good buy I thought this
house was. The remark had been overheard by the current tenants, one of

whom was the owner's daughter. She promptly reported my comment to her parents, encouraging them to demand the full price, as it seemed reasonably certain that if pressed I would pay more than I had offered. My agent tried to convince them they were making a mistake in a rather depressed housing market (and in fact the house did not sell until the following spring). I was offended by the impropriety of their belated repudiation of a legitimately concluded deal and took it as a signal to explore other options, even though my return flight left me only one more day for my search. Early the next morning I revisited a house I had already looked at in a semi-rural area known as Pasadena Park seven miles east of town. The one-acre property at 9708 East Maringo Drive was located directly on the Spokane River and was zoned for small-scale farming, which meant I would be able belatedly to make good on my promise to Trina many years before to buy her a horse when she turned ten (a date that at the time had seemed safely in the distant future). But what really clinched my decision to buy the house was seeing a mallard take off from the scenic river in the early-morning fog. This evidence of rusticity so close to town seemed too good to pass up even though it would lengthen my commute to at least twenty minutes each way. Fortunately, we had just enough savings to make the required $8,000 down payment on the $40,000 house.

When I returned to Spokane with Trina in late August in time for the start of school (Steffi and Nicky were once again to follow at the end of October), I realized what poor condition the house I had so impulsively bought was in. Apparently the previous renters, forced to move out when the house was put up for sale, had taken their revenge on the landlord by destroying two of the toilets in the house and doing much other damage besides, most of it not immediately visible. The landlord did agree to replace one of the toilets, but most of the damage did not come to light until some time had passed. Trina, however, helped me get over my discouragement by her evident delight in the property. "This place is great," she exulted; "there's lots of sawdust in the barn!" Steffi's reaction, when she finally joined us in Spokane in the fall, was less positive: "This is not a house I can be proud of." Its dimensions paled in comparison to our Victorian Irasburg home, but it did have lots of tiny rooms, one of which we converted into Steffi's *Werkstatt*. The children slept in the two upstairs bedrooms, which adults could only reach by ducking down very low at the head of the stairs. Detracting from the otherwise rather idyllic location was the Inland Empire Paper factory about

Thatcher as Europe's first woman prime minister in May 1979. Elected on the promise of cutting taxes, restraining unions, and dismantling the welfare state, her popular libertarian motto was "free choice is what ultimately life is about." Never mind that a totally unregulated market inevitably meant support for the rich at the expense of the poor. In January 1979 the Shah of Iran had been forced to flee a popular Islamic insurgency after 37 years of brutal U.S.-supported dictatorship. In July the dictator Anastasio Somoza, whose family had ruled Nicaragua with American backing since 1933, was ousted by the left-leaning Sandanista revolution. A powerful insurgency was threatening the repressive American-supported military dictatorship in El Salvador as well. Carter did enjoy some transient successes, chief of which were the peace accords between Egypt and Israel negotiated at Camp David (though the results brought no relief to the Palestinians in the occupied territories) and the signing of the SALT II arms control treaty with the USSR (though the failure of the Senate to ratify the treaty meant that it never officially went into effect). The crowning blows to Carter's popularity and prestige came in the fall of the year. In late October 1979, his administration granted shelter to the Shah in the United States to seek medical treatment for an as yet unknown disease that turned out to be terminal cancer. In furious retaliation, revolutionary students seized the American embassy in Teheran with support from the Khomeini regime, taking fifty-two hostages who were not released until the day of Reagan's inauguration in January 1981. Meanwhile, an effort to free the hostages by military means failed badly in April 1980, further throwing Carter's leadership into question. But the crucial blow to Carter's reelection was probably the Soviet invasion of neighboring Afghanistan in December 1979. Carter immediately toughened his cold war stance, going so far as to invoke a boycott of the Moscow Olympics in the summer of 1980. In toughness, however, Carter could never compete with his Republican rivals. In an effort to drive the Soviets out of Afghanistan the Carter and Reagan administrations also mobilized and armed the very same anti-American Islamic fundamentalists who would later launch a world-wide "jihad" against the United States.

Our move to Spokane did not alleviate the strains in our marriage, which paralleled the nation's political decline. There may have been some truth to Tolstoy's famous remark in *Anna Karenina*, to the effect that while all happy families are pretty much alike; all unhappy families are unhappy in different ways. Speaking from my own experience, I can identify neither one specific event nor one specific cause that precipitated the breakdown of our marriage. That it was not of recent vintage, however, became clear to me as early as our year in Burlington in 1970-1971, when I could hardly believe that two people we knew were getting married. "How can anyone *want* to get married?" I thought. "Do they really have any idea what they're getting into?" Steffi later pinned the blame for the breakdown of our marriage on me for wanting a younger woman, but I did not even meet my second wife Sally until six months after our divorce became final in April, 1983. Infidelity certainly did play a part in our break-up, but we were probably about equally guilty on that score and it has never become entirely clear who took the first misstep (which already occurred in Germany). Suffice it to say that there was no single act of infidelity on either part that can bear the brunt of blame for our parting. More important was a basic incompatibility that came out in a number of ways, not least in escalating mutual recriminations. We were different in many ways, differences that only surfaced or only caused friction over time. One example was in the way we made our living. Steffi was a craftsman with a strong aesthetic sense, which from her perspective I entirely lacked. She did not like intellectuals, preferring artists or people who worked with their hands. This was a sentiment reinforced by her sister Ulrike who referred to me (when I was out of earshot) as "that intellectual asshole". When Steffi first met Sally in the late eighties, before Sally and I were married, Steffi warned her that I was "all brain and no body." Steffi didn't particularly like the Jesuits, either, and accused me of kowtowing to them. Like a true artist she valued independence above all, and some of her criticisms of the Jesuits were actually quite well taken.

> "*Das Leben der Pater ist falsch* (the fathers' life is false). They look for a secure niche in the Church. But life is not like that; life is struggle."

Steffi even offered to set me free to pursue a career in the Church: "Do you want to become a priest? I'll gladly separate from you to give you the opportunity." To my chagrin, even Mama seemed to suspect me of wanting to return to my wartime Catholic roots—for opportunistic reasons. I, on the other hand, thought I had been hired by Gonzaga to reaffirm and strengthen their links to the larger secular academic community from which I had been recruited and in which I had originally hoped to find an institutional home. Nonetheless I was always aware of a certain underlying tension: would I succeed in giving Jesuit education a more liberal turn, or would the Jesuits succeed in making me more religious? The contemplative life had an undeniable appeal.

Reinforcing our differences, Steffi was very gregarious and found it difficult to be alone, whereas I had few close friends and enjoyed my solitude. In the final analysis it may have been simply our living arrangements that made divorce too easy to forego. With two houses 2,500 miles apart the opportunity to split was simply too great. Our dispute rested on what on 9 March 1981 I diagnosed as a mutual charade:

> Steffi's claim that she wants me to give up my job and move to Vermont
> and my claim that I want her to give up Vermont (sell the house) and
> move here. For reasons of self-vindication we must invent the myth that
> separation is the other person's choice alone.

In the end I was no doubt mainly to blame, because I welcomed the split, while Steffi regretted it (or at least that's what she said).

As is undoubtedly true in most failed marriages, infidelities were more a sign that something was wrong in the marriage than the actual cause of the final break. One obvious sign that something was wrong was a development in the spring of 1979 that took me quite by surprise. I fell in love with one of my students. I had been attracted to students before, and would not wish to deny that there is a benign erotic-charismatic component to most good teaching (in one of his books the always provocative Paul Goodman claimed that one of the great perks of college teaching was to be able to spend so much time around vivacious, intelligent, good-looking young people), but this was something else. Toward the end of my course on twentieth-century Europe in spring 1979 one of my students—let's call her Kaye—started attending my office hours with suspicious frequency. What really caught my attention was the fact that she had no hesitation admitting she had not read one of the assigned readings in my class. This struck me as a rather risky way of gaining an instructor's attention, but I couldn't help admiring the seeming indifference to grades that her ready confession implied. In fact, however, she was an A student, who wrote an outstanding final exam in the course and got all A's in her other courses as well. I was flattered to learn that her greatest motivation to excel in my class was to live up to my expectations by showing me what she was capable of! When Steffi had returned to Irasburg in the spring (I had to wait around for the end of Trina's school year before driving back to Vermont) I invited Kaye to visit me at home after the end of the semester. She was a basketball cheerleader and a state beauty queen, the kind of girl I would never have suspected of having the slightest interest in me, but to my delight she was evidently quite taken by me as well—although I suspected it was more the challenge of getting a professor to come down from his high horse that provided her incentive. She was beautiful, sensitive, and intelligent—the ideal student. Above all she represented youth to me, the youth I no longer possessed. I was also very taken by her insistence that age difference makes absolutely no difference when two people are in love. I could not resist fantasizing about having a beautiful wife who actually appreciated intellectual people and was open to tutelage and instruction. For a while I was infatuated enough to believe that a student-teacher relationship was the perfect match (and this at a time when the equal rights amendment and the corrosive effects of power imbalances in personal relationships were everywhere being debated)!. No doubt this was for me the start of a mid-life crisis that culminated in my separation from Steffi in 1981. Kaye and I were well aware of the risks we were running—especially me, as a romance between teacher and student was an absolute no-no at Gonzaga, regardless whether it occurred inside or outside the halls of academe. In the end the romance did not last beyond a week or two that spring and remained mostly in my mind. But I cannot deny its strong emotional impact. As absence makes the heart grow fonder, so my infatuation reached its height in Irasburg in the summer of 1979. I could not believe the ending of some television show in which the hero magnanimously foreswore a certain romantic relationship for what seemed to me to be utterly conventional and insufficient reasons. Virtue triumphing over love because social mores demanded it—is that even remotely credible? I could not help thinking of something I had read somewhere by Bertrand Russell: "Nothing leads more certainly to unhappiness than lack of courage in love."

Steffi and I resumed our cross-country shuttle in academic year 1979-1980, Steffi as usual arriving at the end of October and returning to Vermont with Nick in May. Trina stayed behind to complete the school year in Spokane. In May 1980, after dropping off Sally and Nicky in Vancouver for the trans-Canada rail trip back to Vermont, I made my first return trip to Germany since 1967 for my father's seventieth birthday. Leaving Trina with the McCuddins, I traveled via Canada, participating in a chess tournament in Vancouver on the way. The timing was fortuitous, as we left Spokane several days before Mount Saint Helens blew its top on May 18th. There had been warning signs for weeks beforehand, but no one expected the strength of the eruption when it occurred. It unexpectedly made my flight to Germany much more comfortable as the clouds of ash from the eruption prevented us from landing to pick up the passengers waiting in Calgary, thus leaving the plane half empty. Most of us had two or three seats on which we could stretch out and even get some sleep.

With Sylvia, Papa, Tante Lulli, Stella, and Stella's husband, Ernie

After returning to Spokane in June, Trina and I drove east, this time accompanied by Gloria McCuddin, who was planning to spend the summer with friends and relatives back east. We also brought along a stray mixed-breed dog by the name of *Bursche* whom we had picked up during the year (or, more accurately, who had picked us up). After dropping off Gloria in Connecticut we headed straight for Olaf's son John's June wedding in Kent, where the rest of the family had gathered as well.

With Steffi at John Stackelberg's wedding in Kent, CT, June 1980

The summer of 1980 marked the crisis of our relationship. It turned out that Steffi had a male counterpart to Kaye in Vermont. Dale was a skilful furniture refinisher, only in his early thirties at the time, but he had struck Steffi's fancy. The relationship had apparently been going on for some time. Whereas I yearned to teach a receptive Kaye about history, literature, and philosophy, Steffi looked forward to learning from Dale the secrets of fine craftsmanship in wood. But Steffi also wanted to give him the confidence he lacked to make something out of himself. Both Steffi and I basked in the admiration of our respective young fans. We thought of them as our muses and protégés, sources of inspiration, full of erotic charm. I found out about Dale when Steffi called him at 3 in the morning one night—I had followed her downstairs and overheard the conversation. Steffi thought I'd be much angrier than I was, but I was full of mixed feelings. Though the Kaye lodestar had dimmed in the past academic year and we had not resumed our brief romance, she was still very much in my thoughts, as I imagine Dale was in Steffi's. Was this our opportunity to go our separate ways? I knew it would be hard on the children, now fourteen and nine, respectively.

Trina and Nick in Spokane, 1980

We decided to stay together for at least one more year. Trina was an extremely bright student going into her last year in junior high school in the fall of 1980. We decided it was our duty to do whatever we could to further her education. In July 1980 I took her to Concord, New Hampshire, to interview for admission to St. Paul's, where Olaf and I had gone to school from 1946 to 1948, and which now was open to girls as well. However, Trina adamantly insisted on attending a school that had a horseback riding program, something St. Paul's did not have at the time. When I tried to console her for the lack of riding at St. Paul's by telling her of the many other available activities, she replied, "would you want to switch from chess to checkers?" She ended up being accepted at Kent School in Connecticut, another prestigious preparatory school now open to girls, where she was to enter the fourth form (tenth grade) in fall 1981. If Steffi and I were going to separate, it made sense to do so at that point. Trina had already made it clear that she did not want to live with either of us. In my journal I wrote: "Trina playing both sides against each other as a means of *legitimately* asserting her independence—for who can blame her for refusing to live with quarreling parents?"

The summer of 1980 was an emotional roller-coaster ride for the entire family with lots of ups and downs, bickering and caustic exchanges. Neither Steffi nor I were sure what we wanted to do, although each of us insisted that whatever decision we came to, it would be our own. "*Ich bin hin und hergerissen* (I'm torn back and forth)" Steffi told me, "not between two men but between two ways of life (*Lebeweisen*)." Both of us felt increasingly hemmed in by our failing marriage. My condition for staying together another year was for Steffi to accompany me back to Spokane in August. I did not want to leave Steffi on her own in Vermont for another two months as in the past. This is the way I put it in my journal on July 15th:

> Taking Steffi along in August: the obvious motive is vanity—to show that I can do it. But perhaps there is a more subtle motive as well: to insure that the break, when it occurs, is final: to prevent Steffi from following after (for instance, by arrangement with Gloria, who would pick her up in Calgary) thereby perpetuating the lifestyle she would prefer: six months here, six months there, with a lover in every port.

All summer we argued about whether Steffi should come to Spokane in August or whether we should call it quits right then. Our problematic marriage was the talk of the family that summer. Mama actually commented on how much friendlier Steffi had unexpectedly become to her. Steffi even noticed a change in herself. "I'm full of love this summer. I want to embrace everyone." But Mama was critical of Betsy who first told Mama about Steffi's romance: "It's slightly pornographic to see those kinds of things. Betsy is interested in that kind of thing." But then she conceded: "It *is* interesting." I had been concerned that Mama would try to persuade me not to abandon the marriage, but in fact the opposite was the case. "If Steffi really believes all the things she says about you, I don't see how you can continue to live with her. "

Mama in Vermont, summer 1980

As it happened, Steffi's entire family, mother, step-father, and sister (Ulrike and her boyfriend Nick Plein had bought some property in Vermont), visited us that summer and were very much witnesses to the drama.

> The matter-of-fact way in which Steffi's mother and Hans have accepted the situation, as if prepared well beforehand (through Steffi's letters?). Their reaction has been only an increased sense of proprietorship over the house, as with total impunity they now plan restorations and remodeling without once thinking it might be necessary to consult me.

Ulrike's and Nick Plein's property in Vermont, 1980

When Steffi asked her mother for advice what to do in her dilemma, Lilo was noncommittal: "Choose Dale," she said," only if he is an improvement over what you have." But unwittingly she encouraged Steffi's indecision by admitting, *"Ich traue keinem Mann mehr* (I no longer trust any man)." Steffi even sought the advice of my friend and former roommate, the psychiatrist Paul Russell, who practiced in Boston and occasionally came to see us in Vermont with his girlfriend Franny: "I want to ask Paul whether leading a double life can make one sick," Steffi said. I had earlier written Paul about Kaye. "That was a powerful letter," he told me later, immediately making me regret that I had not had the courage to send the letter to Kaye instead. Even Trina got into the discussion by citing for me a slogan that hung in her school: "If you love something, set it free. If it comes back to you, it's yours. If it doesn't, it never was yours anyway." Trina later told me that at the time she had thought the term "nuclear family" referred to its potential for explosion. I was working on a paper on Nietzsche that summer. Steffi attributed my bad moods to the influence of *"diesen Weiberhasser* (this woman-hater)."

But reading Nietzsche was a solace to me, especially this pronouncement by Zarathustra: "*Wohl brach ich die Ehe—aber zuerst brach die Ehe—mich* (true, I broke the marriage—but first the marriage broke—me)!" I also rather liked his analysis of why some women hated men:

> *Also sprach das Eisen zum Magneten: „Ich hasse dich am meisten, weil du anziehst aber nicht stark genug bist an dich zu ziehen."* Thus spake the iron to the magnet: „I hate you the most, because you attract, but are not strong enough to draw [me] to you."

The academic year 1980-1981 was our final year together. The coming separation gave all our activities that year a wistful, melancholy quality, but my mind was made up. I did not know what the future would hold, but I knew I wanted a change and was determined to seize what would very likely be my last opportunity. Steffi was more ambivalent, mainly because in that fateful summer of 1980 Dale had not exhibited the level of enthusiasm for and commitment to their relationship that she had hoped for or expected. Falling for weak and passive men seemed to be her unenviable fate.

9

THE STRUGGLE FOR TENURE, 1981-1982

I received two years' credit for my experience as Assistant Visiting Professor at Oregon and South Dakota, so I went up early for tenure in academic year 1981-1982. Having been promoted to Associate Professor after the acceptance for publication of my book, *Idealism Debased: From Völkisch Ideology to National Socialism* by Kent State University Press the previous year, my prospects looked very good indeed. As John Sisk of the English Department—probably the best-known Gonzaga faculty member and the one most respected for his scholarship—told me: "They can't very well promote you one year and then refuse you tenure the next." I should perhaps have been forewarned, though, by my colleague Bob Carriker's unexpectedly hostile reaction when I told him I was applying for promotion in fall 1980: "Isn't that a bit arrogant of you?" Carriker had also written personally to the president of the university complaining that I had gotten a bigger raise than he after the publication of my book. But Carriker had a college-wide reputation for easily feeling threatened by his colleagues and preferring a steady turnover of junior faculty, so I wasn't particularly worried, especially since I had been reappointed every year, including in spring 1981, with glowing recommendations and without any departmental reservations. Every year the dean had personally come to my office to tell me that the administration was very pleased with my teaching evaluations and professional publications and expressed the hope that I would continue my good work at Gonzaga. Moreover, the Academic Vice President, Fr. Peter Ely, had asked me to participate in the founding of a new International Studies Program at Gonzaga that went into operation in the fall of 1981, and he had appointed me its director. I had already represented the university at a number of meetings of the newly-founded Pacific Northwest Consortium for International Education based in Seattle. I had even represented the University President, Fr. Barney Coughlin, at a meeting of the presidents of Jesuit Universities on the subject of international studies.

There was a little hiccup in the faculty's acceptance of the U.S. Department of Education grant for the establishment of an international studies program that I had helped to write. The Academic Council at first voted to reject the grant, but this was based less on opposition to the new International Studies Program than on friction between faculty and administration on decision-making and governance and especially on some faculty members' fears that international studies was being funded at the expense of faculty salaries (not entirely unfounded, since the grant did call for matching university funding). Fr. Ely had asked me to make the case for the grant to the Academic Council, so I could not help but take their initial rejection a bit personally. However, numerous members of the Council came up to me later and apologized for their vote and explained that it had nothing to do with me. On a second vote the following day, the Academic Council reversed itself and the grant was accepted by an overwhelming margin. I knew Carriker (who was not on the partly elected and partly appointed Academic Council) didn't like my prominent role in the International Studies Program, which gave me a semi-independent base outside the department. But he claimed that his opposition to the International Studies Program was only because he wanted me for the history department one-hundred percent.

My scholarly credentials could hardly be impugned. My book, *Idealism Debased: From Völkisch Ideology to National Socialism*, based on my dissertation, was published by the Kent State University Press in 1981. In October 1979 I had begun presenting papers at the annual meetings of the newly-founded German Studies Association (GSA—then still known as the Western Association for German Studies). I had learned about this organization from the Germanist Karen Achberger while I was still at Oregon. The conference in 1979 was held on the campus of Stanford University, allowing me to visit my Harvard roommate Paul Russell's sister Arlie Hochschildt, whom I had not seen for more than twenty years. Arlie was now a successful sociologist at Berkeley and was soon to achieve considerable acclaim for a number of widely-publicized studies on women and work. She and her husband Adam owned a lovely home in the Castro district of San Francisco. I soon found myself in a lively dialogue with

Adam in which I defended, to my later embarrassment, the Soviet experiment in socialism despite all its obvious faults. Adam Hochschildt, who had recently returned from a visit to the USSR, set me straight on the reality of repression in that country, but I wasn't yet prepared to give up on the 1960s dream of a democratic socialism and thought at the time that the best way of supporting this goal was to keep the Soviet experiment going. It seemed to me that Adam Hochschildt's criticism of the Soviet Union presaged the very deliberate revival of the cold war by President Ronald Reagan the following year (of which Hochschildt, the founding editor of *Mother Jones*, was to be duly critical). My journal entries reflected my point of view:

9 Jan, 1980 It is incredible that people don't recognize that something must be wrong when the killers of SALT II, the apostles of nuclear armament, gloat at the "rape of Afghanistan." Finally a reason for their intransigence! Things are going *their* way!

27 Jan, 1980 The difference between our and the Russian "fathers of the H-bomb": Again the Russians have us beat. [Edward] Teller is paving the ground for its use, [Andrey] Sakharove tries to prevent it.

17 April, 1980 Fears of a Soviet nuclear strike, insofar as they are genuine, and all evidence points to the fact that they are not, but that they are professed for ideological reasons—so obviously a projection of our own aggressive impulses as to be almost obscene. Based on a total *Verkennung* (misreading) of Soviet socialism. Their confidence is so strong that they would never jeopardize their budding system by waging an aggressive war; for the only thing that can destroy socialism now is a war that destroys *everything*. We, unfortunately, have none of that confidence—only a propped-up righteousness based on self-interest, the interest of maintaining economic dominance. Hence our obsession with the *threat* of socialism, which translates into a readiness to destroy it at the first opportunity. Only we have good reason to use force, because we feel in our bones that time is *not* on our side.

16 Jun, 1980 Olaf's attitude, such a barometer of American values, on our policy toward the Soviet Union proving that he—and indeed

America—have learned nothing from Vietnam. "Where would *you* draw the line on Soviet aggression?" he asked.

18 Jun, 1980 To those who propagate the 1914 thesis drawing parallels between the U.S.S.R. and Imperial Germany (encirclement theory, preventive war, etc.), I want to say: Grown men and women, behaving like children in your righteousness and self-delusion! The parallel is there—but it is *you* who are behaving like the Imperial German leadership. It is you who can't be trusted. It is you who fear for your wealth and privileges and see enemies all around you.

19 Jun, 1980 We should ask ourselves: why do we *want* the experiment in communism to fail? Even if our criticisms are well-taken, why should we not hope that this experiment in communal living will eventually succeed? The charge that communism leads to the formation of a power elite is true enough. But we certainly can't argue, given our values, that providing incentives or rewards to those who "make it" by contributing to the system's success is wrong. If we accepted as our basic premise that a well-functioning communal society is desirable, we would see nothing wrong with an arrangement that rewards efforts to work toward its achievement.

27 Jun, 1980 Why isn't it obvious to all that the re-intensification, the real cause of the revival, of the Cold War is America's frustrated response to its disastrous failure in Iran?

28 Jun, 1980 I have this feeling about America: what if the brakes give out? At the moment they still seem to be adequate. There are enough persons of integrity and sense scattered around to dampen the fervors of chauvinism.

28 July, 1980 The irony is that socialism will gain appeal in the U.S. precisely *for* its repressive qualities.

6 Sep, 1980 It is not, as [Daniel] Moynihan maintained, that we must be afraid of the younger generation of Russians, who no longer remember World War II and pursue the hope of Russian supremacy, but that we

must be afraid of the older generation of Americans, who cannot forget World War II and the era of American supremacy.

20 Dec, 1980 There is a dialectic at work that makes socialists the most individualistic of people and "individualists" the most conformist and colorless.

31 Aug, 1981 The Soviet threat to the U.S. is one of ideas and values; the American threat to Russia is one of arms and power.

3 Dec, 1981 If religion *is* the grounds for attacking communism, then communism has grounds for suppressing religion.

4 Jan, 1982 We don't have any agreed-upon standard of measurement of human misery. But who is to say that it is less in this country than in the U.S.S.R.?

16 Jan, 1982 Life under communism: when you have set yourself the goal of taking care of *everyone*, you cannot allow the same leeway for *prima donnas* as in a liberal society in which everyone is free to go to the dogs.

24 Jan, 1982 What we accuse the communists of—superficial, distorted, "censored" reporting—we are guilty of. [The Coeur d'Alene-based silver mining company] Bunker Hill as a case in point: although it is an obvious case of callous exploitation—the workers are simply cast off, having completed their usefulness—the union is made the scapegoat. Every gain the unions have been able to obtain for workers is portrayed as an obstacle to full employment. Workers are encouraged to express their outrage at the union. In a communist country Bunker Hill would have been kept in operation even at very marginal profitability. That is why their economy "stagnates," but the needs of their citizenry are met. If communism disappeared from the earth, millions would be left to face poverty without anyone to take their side. To understand communist repression one must realize that to them bourgeois traits—acquisitiveness, aggressiveness, self-seeking—are criminal traits, and bourgeois freedoms merely the climate that tolerates criminality. We consider it a world turned upside down; they consider it a world turned right side up.

To me it seemed clear. The New Cold War launched by Ronald Reagan represented the Vietnam hawks getting their belated revenge. Indeed, one of Reagan's major goals was to overcome the "Vietnam syndrome," defined as the reluctance to use American military power to defend the world-wide interests of America's dominant elites.

In the summer of 1981, I participated in a National Endowment for the Humanities (NEH) faculty seminar offered by the noted scholar Henry A. Turner at Yale. Turner had dedicated his scholarly career to defending the liberal capitalist system from its Marxist critics. At the time of the seminar he was hard at work on his *opus magnum, Big Business and the Rise of Hitler.* If the Marxists were right and capitalists were responsible for the rise of fascism, Turner said, then capitalism stood condemned by history. This was not a conclusion Turner was prepared to accept. He preferred to emphasize the anti-modern and anti-capitalist features of fascism. He did, however, appreciate my book *Idealism Debased,* perhaps because I stressed ideology rather than economics. We did a lot of good-natured sparring in the seminar, where I gained the reputation of resident leftist. I did score one point when I forced Turner and his assistant William Patch, a specialist on the government of Heinrich Brüning, to concede that the Nazis were anti-union. A surprising number of seminar participants seemed unaware or unwilling to acknowledge that the Nazis were strongly anti-labor.

A seminar outing at Yale, summer 1981

The publication of Turner's book was delayed by the appearance of David Abraham's Marxist analysis of *The Collapse of the Weimar Republic* in 1983. Turner assailed Abraham's book as well as its author, whom he accused of deliberately falsifying the facts. And indeed, the book was replete with errors of translation and transcription, the result of carelessness and sloppiness rather than any intention to deceive. But Abraham's inaccuracies gave Turner the chance to evade all discussion of interpretation and methodology, where the real differences between the two scholars lay. Turner's rigorously positivist approach was suspicious of explanatory conceptualizations, especially ones that were critical of existing economic relations. He found in his research that business people had indeed contributed substantial sums to the Nazis, but he attributed their largesse not to sympathy for Nazi goals, but to their understandable wish to be prepared for the contingency of the Nazis' coming to power. The campaign against Abraham was successful. He lost his teaching position at Princeton and was effectively blacklisted within the historical profession for a time, despite the publication of a corrected version of his book a few years later.

Of course, the political shift to the right in the 1980s could not help but have an effect on my tenure decision as well. It strengthened the conservative political forces in the university, as it strengthened the religious right in the nation as a whole. They could not get me on professional criteria, but they could attack me on ideological grounds. Was I really in tune with Gonzaga's uniquely Catholic mission? As long as social justice was the Jesuits' primary goal, as indeed it was during the 1970s, no one could accuse me of failing to represent that mission. But once priority shifted to reaffirming Catholic orthodoxy through the primacy of faith and strengthening the institutional authority of the Church—as it did at least to some degree with the more general shift to the right in the 1980s—I became vulnerable to charges of misunderstanding the "unique mission of Gonzaga University." Two of the three senior (i.e., tenured) members of the department were political and religious conservatives. They identified me, not inaccurately, as a "secular humanist," who eventually might try through curricular and personnel decisions to recreate the department in his own image. Their objective was to counter that danger by denying me tenure. And they almost succeeded.

However, I did have on my side the third tenured member and only woman in the department, Betsy Downey, who had replaced Fr. Via as chair and fiercely and effectively campaigned on my behalf. Fr. Via had been reassigned to direct the Gonzaga-in-Florence program and did not take part in the tenure decision, which probably worked to my disadvantage, as Fr. Via was quite aware of Carriker's bullying tendencies and helped to keep them in check (as did Carriker's wife Eleanor). Ultimately the crucial factor was that the administration, including the president and academic vice president, had a vested interest in my success and continued service at Gonzaga. And there were many others rooting for me as well. Tony Wadden, my colleague in the English Department, called the opposition to my tenure "embarrassing." My student Thad Lightfoot was the first person to inform me that the Rank and Tenure Committee had failed to recommend me for tenure. He had heard of this decision through a back-channel source at Jesuit House. All the bad news reached me while I was visiting Olaf in Kent, Ohio, on my return flight from an international studies conference in Cincinnati in February or March 1982. Olaf had left Duke in 1976 to become head of the mathematics department at Kent State University for the next twenty years.

The vote on my application for tenure had been tied three to three in the Rank and Tenure Committee, leaving the decision to the *ex officio* chair, the Academic Vice President. On my return to Spokane Fr. Ely called me into his office and began by explaining to me that the university was legally entitled to make personnel decisions purely on religious grounds. He said that there was some concern that I was not only non-religious, but perhaps even anti-religious. He said he didn't think this was the case, but he needed some corroboration from me. I told him I considered myself religious in the sense of being extremely interested in and concerned about the "Big Questions"—questions about the meaning of life and the nature of the universe. He graciously accepted my rather forced explanation. My tenure application was approved.

What I really thought about religion I confided only to my journal:

Feb 27 1979 The Church in an atmosphere of tolerance is so much more attractive than in a climate of orthodoxy, because in the former instance you know people become priests and nuns because they really believe, rather than for career or power.

Nov 28 1982 Perhaps in religion the question really is, do we take time out to ingratiate ourselves with God or do we go about His work quietly, steadily, using all our faculties, guided by the inborn compass that presumably He has given us. In that sense dogma *is* an obstacle to true religion. True religion defined: awareness of the mystery of the universe *without* brown-nosing. Can we live any more religiously than we do when we constantly overcome self? And that includes overcoming the selfishness of...religion.

That spring of 1982 was one of the happiest and most exhilarating periods of my life. I finally had a secure position doing what I did best and enjoyed most, namely, writing and teaching. Trina spent her spring vacation from Kent School in Spokane, keeping Nick company and seeing all her old friends while I traveled to Vancouver to give guest lectures on Nietzsche and Nazism at the University of British Columbia and Simon Fraser University at the invitation of Ted Hill and Martin Kitchen, respectively.

Trina in Spokane for spring vacation, 1982

Trina had enjoyed a marvelous send-off from Spokane after her graduation from Argonne Junior High School in June 1981. About a dozen of her classmates had come to our house before 7 in the morning to bid her goodbye. It was a dramatic demonstration of how well she was liked by her classmates.

Trina's fifteenth birthday party, April 1981

In August 1981 I set out with Nick and our dog *Bursche* on our return trip to Spokane via the Black Hills of South Dakota and Mount Rushmore.

Nick with *Bursche* at Mt. Rushmore, August 1981

Nick had wanted to continue his schooling in Spokane, and I welcomed the challenge of single-parenting, a challenge faced much more often by women than by men.

Nick, Christmas 1982

However, despite my best efforts to arrange a convenient schedule, Nick was a latchkey kid, arriving home from school about an hour before me. He had difficulty controlling *Bursche*, who loved to bark and chase our neighbor's horses. Eventually I was forced to have *Bursche* put down, to the consternation of my colleague in philosophy Mike Matthis, and especially his wife Rose, who found my action unbelievably callous. But I really had no choice under the circumstances.

Colleagues Mike Matthis and Franz Schneider at our home on Maringo Drive

To top off the splendid academic year 1981-1982, I received a Fulbright grant to attend a five-week seminar for faculty in Germany in summer 1982, while Nick spent the summer with his mother in Irasburg. The first three weeks of the seminar were spent in Bonn, at that time still the capital of West Germany, and the last two weeks in the still divided city of Berlin, a kind of homecoming for me. We were the first American group, we were later told, who spoke only German with each other, never lapsing into English. Later seminar groups followed our example. My colleague from the University of Arkansas, Todd Hanlin, and I set the tone to such a degree that some people referred to our seminar as the "Rod and Todd show."

Fulbright Seminar, summer 1982

With Todd Hanlin, 1982

Our colleague Peter Nutting, at that time still at Cornell, was a peace activist who got us to participate in several anti-nuclear demonstrations.

Peter Nutting, 1982

Later that summer we celebrated Mama's seventieth and Olaf's fiftieth birthdays. Mama demonstrated her youthfulness by standing on her head!

Mama standing on her head at her seventieth birthday party, 1982

Steffi and I made one last, half-hearted effort at reconciliation in the summer of 1982, but it was no good. Tenure and the prospect of an extended stay in Spokane made me want to start a new life without the burden of an unhappy wife. Final separation and divorce was very painful for both of us. In fact, Steffi threatened to fight the divorce all the way, but fortunately for me, she fell in love with a fellow patient in an alcohol-addiction treatment program in which she enrolled in late 1982. I missed her very much for quite a while, but derived strength from Oscar Wilde's paradoxical aesthetic dictum, "One must always seek the most tragic."

Epilogue

In retrospect, this volume could well have been entitled, *My Midlife Crisis*. It described the breakdown of my marriage, which had begun so promisingly. It also described my professional woes as I gave up my dreams of becoming a writer in favor of a new career as a college teacher. My long and at times frustrating search for employment contributed to my marital troubles, but ultimately ended happily with a tenured position at Gonzaga University and a new home in Spokane. The final volume of my memoirs, if time allows me to complete them, will deal with my long and satisfying career at Gonzaga and my happy marriage to my soul-mate Sally Winkle, Director of Women's and Gender Studies and Professor of German Language and Literature at Eastern Washington University.